Best wishes!

Howard Buffett

SPOTS BEFORE YOUR EYES
Cheetahs of Africa

Spots

Before

Your

Eyes

Foreword
Dr. Jane Goodall

Photographs
Howard G. Buffett
and
Ann van Dyk

THIS BOOK IS DEDICATED TO DEVON
FOR HER HELP, SUPPORT AND UNDERSTANDING.

ISBN 0-9707385-6-0
Library of Congress Card Number 2002116769

Printed by
Tien Wah Press (Pte) Limited
4 Pandan Crescent Singapore
Image Reproduction by Allied Photocolor

Published by BioImages
P.O. Box 4537
Decatur, IL 62525
Email: BioImages@aol.com
Fax: 217.429.0206
Or
The De Wildt Cheetah and Wildlife Trust
P.O. Box 1756
Hartbeespoort
0216
South Africa
Phone: 011.27.12.504.1556
Fax: 011.27.12.504.1921
Email: cheetah@dewildt.org.za
www.dewildt.org.za

Production costs donated by The Howard G. Buffett Foundation
All proceeds benefit The De Wildt Cheetah and Wildlife Trust and the International Cheetah Conservation Foundation

ACKNOWLEDGEMENTS

A number of people made it possible for us to produce this book. Several individuals, through skill and commitment, helped provide the opportunity to capture many of these images on film, and others contributed important information. Without the help of those listed below, we could not have completed this book.

A sincere thank you to the following:

Jill Bauer, Annie Beckhelling and Cheetah Outreach, Vanessa Bouwer, Peter and Jennifer Buffett, Deon Cilliers, Derek Craighead, John Craighead, Marilyn Dean, Dr. Sarah Durant, Linda Fultz, Fraser Grear, Dawn Glorer, Andene Grobler, Scott Hawbaker, Tracy and Jim Hill, Garth Hovell, Kara Hubner, Paul Laing, Bob Little and Allied Photocolor, Anton Louw, Schalk van der Merwe, Heidi Möeller, Andre Neuhoff, Christo van Niekerk, Bruce Ochse, Doug Oller, Kevin Pretorius, Thiele Robinson, Liesl Smith, Dr. Alan Turner, Dr. Blaire van Valkenburgh, Nölene Venter, Kelly Wilson, Carola Zardo, the staff of The De Wildt Cheetah and Wildlife Centre and the Nature Conservation Department of the Limpopo Province, South Africa.

A special thank you to Derek Books, Devon Buffett, Howard W. Buffett, Dr. Jane Goodall, Cynthia Kemp, Peter and Penny Kinnear, Tom Mangelsen, and Alan Strachan.

MENU

FOREWORD

DR. JANE GOODALL

© Howard G. Buffett

I can still remember the first cheetah I saw. It was way back in 1958 when I was working on a 'dig' at Olduvai (now Oldupai) Gorge with the late Louis Leakey, and his wife Mary, and Gillian, another young assistant like me. We were searching for proof that prehistoric man had once roamed the Serengeti plains, as Louis and Mary believed. Eventually they were proved right, but at that time no human remains had been found, and the now famous paleontological site was unknown. We were surrounded by absolutely wild country, the Africa I had dreamed of as a child growing up in England. And every evening, after the hard work of digging under the hot African sun, Gillian and I were allowed to wander off on the plains.

There were no roads. The only trails were made by the many animals who lived there. As we roamed through the acacia growing along the edge of the gorge we met Grant's gazelles and diminutive dik diks, giraffes and ostriches, mongooses and lizards. One evening there was a rhino. He knew something strange was around but with his poor eyesight and without the benefit of our scent (which was, luckily for us, being blown away from him) he was confused. After trotting back and forth with head held high and tail in the air, like an overgrown warthog, he tetchily made off. It was even more exciting when a young male lion followed us for at least two hundred yards. He was simply curious - he had never seen anything like us in his life. He might have seen an occasional Masai warrior - although we saw them only a few times during our three month stay. Evidently he decided we were not very interesting for after what seemed an eternity he left us and went about his business.

And then there was the cheetah. He was standing on a a slight rise, silhouetted against the evening sky. He was staring so intently at something in the grass ahead that he never realized two strangers from another world were gazing at him in wonder. He was so beautiful. And then suddenly he was gone. One moment he was standing there, head held high and long tail just twitching at the tip, and the next instant he stepped down and vanished into the golden grass of the Serengeti. It was not until much later that I watched a cheetah hunting and saw the incredible speed and awesome grace of the lovely cat in action.

Those days at Olduvai were among the most enchanted of my life to be so surrounded by animals in an Africa that was still so unspoiled. By 1967, just ten years later, everything had changed. There were still quite a lot of animals, for it is protected as a Conservation Area, but there seemed to be fewer and there were no rhinos - every single one had been poached for its horn. There were roads cutting through the Gorge, and facilities for tourists. It was tamed.

And now, as we move through the early years of a new century, the situation for animals across Africa - and almost everywhere else in the world - has become very grim indeed. Wild habitats shrink as human populations grow, needing ever more land to grow their crops and feed their livestock. Trees are cut for firewood, for building poles, for charcoal to sell. Soil erosion gets ever worse and gradually desert-like conditions claim more and more of the land. Animals are hunted for food or body parts, caught in traps or simply die of starvation as human competitors seize the best remaining places to live. Thousands are captured for the live animal trade, taken from their homes and sold for a variety of purposes - for pets, zoos, entertainment or medical research. More and more animals are listed in the IUCN Red Data book, first as threatened and then endangered. Like chimpanzees. Like cheetahs.

Even in places where they are supposedly protected (unless those places are very large, comprising whole ecosystems, and very well patrolled) the natural balance between predator and prey, between the animals and their habitat, is inevitably disturbed. And once this happens all kinds of things go wrong. For example, when elephants move into protected areas to escape the pressure of hunting, the trees suffer, along with all the creatures that depend on them, and conditions become increasingly arid. Lions, similarly, may be confined within an unusually small range for their species. Competition - both between the lions and other predators - increases, especially when the prey population is poached or shot illegally for human consumption. Cheetahs cannot compete with lions, nor with packs of hyenas, and they tend to get pushed to the edge of the smaller parks or other such areas of wilderness where they come into constant conflict with humans. Cheetahs are one of the most endangered predators in Africa today.

A major problem facing the larger animals is the fragmentation of their habitat. Cut off from others of their kind by human habitation, a small population will become increasingly inbred, decline in numbers and eventually become locally extinct. This is the very real danger that threatens the chimpanzee population of Gombe National Park that has been studied continuously since 1960. When I first arrived there, the forest habitat stretched for miles along the eastern shore of Lake Tanganyika, all of it inhabited by chimpanzees. Today, outside the tiny thirty square miles of the national park, the trees are gone as a result of human population growth in surrounding areas. The Gombe chimpanzees, numbering less than one-hundred and twenty individuals, are isolated, cut off from other conspecifics by cultivated hillsides on three sides and the lake on the fourth. Unless we are successful in our efforts to link this remnant population to the few remaining fragments of the population to the north, the famous Gombe chimpanzees might eventually die out.

Sometimes entire species become extinct, not only in certain parts of their range, but everywhere. In 2000, a beautiful species of monkey from the rain forests of Ghana, Miss Waldron's Colobus, was declared officially extinct as a result of human activities - hunting and logging. We humans have been responsible for the extinction of passenger pigeons that once darkened the skies of North America in their millions. They were hunted for sport. The dodo was eaten to extinction. And every day small animals and plants, endemic to small ecosystems, become extinct when their habitats are destroyed. Life forms that took millions of years to evolve, along with their genes, are now gone – gone forever.

Of course, countless animals became extinct through causes other than human actions. We were not, after all, responsible for the demise of the dinosaurs! They perished, along with seventy percent of all the species then on Earth, about sixty-five million years ago. But in the last hundred years humans have been the cause of untold animal losses, and global rates of extinction are thought to be the highest they have been since the catastrophe that destroyed the dinosaurs. And, especially in tropical forests, clear cutting undoubtedly causes the extinction of many small seemingly insignificant microbes, plants, insects and so forth even before they are known to science. I agree wholeheartedly with the eminent biologist Ed Wilson who believes that this loss of biodiversity is something future generations will not forgive us for.

But why? Why should we, or our descendants, care? Surely it is more important to boost timber exports, to clear huge areas of land for intensive farming to promote agribusiness profits, than to worry about the loss of some insignificant little weed or creepy crawly, frog or bird? Or even, for that matter, larger and more charismatic animals such as chimpanzees and cheetahs? Thousands of people feel this way, entrenched in the belief that animals are merely on this planet for our good, and that we humans must always come first. How then can we justify our concern for the natural world and the animals who live there?

We can argue that some contact with nature is essential for the healthy development of the human psyche. Forests and savannas, wetlands and mountains, are beautiful and surely need to be part of our world forever. For many, even those who have never had the good fortune to experience truly wild places, just knowing that they still exist is comforting. And the awesome array of animal species who inhabit those places deserve to exist in their own right. For although those raised in the Judea-Christian religion may truly believe that God gave man 'dominion' over all animals, this is based on an incorrect translation of the Hebrew word *v, turdyin* in Genesis Chapter 1 verse 26. Thus when we read that God gave man 'dominion' over the animals, a more correct meaning is 'to rule over as a wise king rules over his subjects, with care and respect'. The word implies a sense of responsibility and enlightened stewardship. Any person who has grown up with, or has come to appreciate the companionship and unconditional love of a dog, cat or some other animal knows that we humans are not the only beings on this planet with personalities, minds capable of solving problems, and feelings similar to those we call happiness and sadness, despair, fear and pain. Research on chimpanzees and other creatures with complex brains has increasingly convinced even scientists that animals are not just animated machines, triggered by internal 'drive' receiving and responding to various external stimuli. In other words, common sense, religion and science all suggest that the amazing animals with whom we share planet Earth deserve our sympathy and protection.

Unfortunately we have already inflicted huge amounts of damage on nature. Perhaps it is too late. Perhaps cheetahs and chimpanzees and the savanas and forest where they live, are already doomed. In some places this may indeed be true. For although, in many countries, steps are being taken to protect the natural world - they are seldom bold enough and sometimes introduced too late. Thus in most countries, although there are laws and regulations regarding the hunting and capture of animals - such as those that make it illegal to hunt during the birth season, or to kill mothers with youngsters or members of an endangered species - these laws are seldom enforced. This is because of lack of money, lack of political will, ignorance - or because of corruption. Typically those employed to enforce such laws in Africa are poorly paid, and often lack equipment of the most basic kind for their sometimes dangerous task. A ranger with no vehicle and one old rifle with little ammunition is often understandably reluctant to confront poachers armed with modern automatic weapons and functioning vehicles. Yet despite this there are many wardens and rangers, those appointed as guardians of wildlife, who risk their lives despite their seemingly hopeless task. I have enormous regard for these men, and feel privileged to have known many of them. They desperately need our help and support.

But however dedicated and courageous, those appointed to preserve the wilderness can never be successful if they are surrounded by people living in abject poverty, people who abuse their environment because they have no choice. If the land they are living on cannot support them as their numbers grow, if they cannot afford to buy food from elsewhere, and if they cannot move to a different area, then they must destroy more and ever more of the remaining habitat to try to feed themselves and their families. They are caught in a vicious cycle of poverty, hunger and disease. They have little chance for education, the women seldom have a voice and family size is often completely unrealistic. The poverty and hunger gets ever worse. And the numbers of people living in these soul destroying conditions are increasing as a result of the ethnic conflicts that rage in so many parts of the world, forcing millions of people away from their homes to seek refuge in places that may already have reached carrying capacity. Now we must add to this the horror and suffering of the AIDS epidemic.

And so, we ask again, can anything be done? This was the question I asked myself when, fifteen years ago, I flew over the Gombe National Park and saw the extent of the deforestation beyond its boundaries. How could these precious chimpanzees be saved when the people in the surrounding countryside, their own growing population swelled by refugees from Burundi and the Congo, were struggling to survive as their land became progressively eroded and barren? This led to the Jane Goodall Institute (JGI) initiating a program to improve the lives of the people living along the shores of Lake Tanganyika and around Gombe National Park. The lake Tanganyika Catchment Agriculture, Reforestation and Education program, TACARE, has been hugely successful. Thirty-three villages now have tree nurseries, and wood lots, and they learn farming methods most suited to their environment. We have established nine micro-credit banks (based on Grameen Bank) that enable small groups (mostly women) to take out very small loans with which to start small environmentally sustainable projects (such as making cooking stoves from local clay that are designed to hugely economize on firewood). Working with the regional medical authorities, the TACARE vehicles deliver primary health care to villagers. Family planning information and AIDS education is made available. Conservation education is provided and groups of older children and adults visit Gombe National Park. We also provide some scholarships for gifted girls to go from primary to secondary school. The reason for our emphasis on empowering women, increasing their education and self esteem, is that it has been shown, around the world, how this leads to a reduction in family size. We also involve the villagers with our research in the park - even some who have only been to primary school. They learn to follow the chimpanzee and record their behavior, sometimes using video cameras. They care about the chimps, are proud of their work, talk about it to the villagers and thus help our conservation education efforts.

As a result, the local people are now prepared to help protect the chimpanzees. And, most exciting, many villages have been persuaded to leave the stumps of trees that they cut down, rather than continually eradicating new growth. Within five years these stumps, if left alone, become twenty to thirty foot trees.

As a result 'TACARE forests' are appearing in many places, boding well for our plan to establish the corridor linking the Gombe chimpanzees to remnant groups north of the park.

TACARE gives two reasons for hope for the future of wildlife conservation: firstly it shows that if you help the local people, gain their trust and improve their education, they will help to protect rather than destroy the environment; secondly, that nature, given a chance, is very resilient. There are many similar programs to help people living around other national parks and reserves throughout the developing world. And it is these programs, along with controlled tourism, that boosts the local economy as well as bringing foreign exchange into the country, that are the best conservation tools.

Another reason for hope lies in the passion and commitment of people like Ann van Dyk. Cheetahs, as mentioned, are highly endangered - but for Ann's project they would be in a far worse plight. I have not yet visited De Wildt where she has worked so hard and selflessly to save the cheetahs, but I have heard glowing reports and I am filled with admiration. And it seems that whenever there is an animal species in a desperate situation, there will be an individual, or a group of individuals who, because they care and because they will not give up, may achieve the seemingly impossible. Margaret Owing, in California, was responsible for the hard-fought campaign that eventually gave protection to the highly endangered Californian Sea Otter. California Condors, Whooping Cranes, and the Seika Deer of Taiwan - all of these species were almost extinct before determined biologists started captive breeding programs that worked. In all three cases there were fewer than twenty individuals remaining in the wild when action was finally taken - each of these species now number, respectively, about one-hundred fifty, two-hundred fifty and four-hundred individuals in the wild. Don Morton, in New Zealand, rescued the Black Robin when the species was represented by just two birds - one male and one female. The task was deemed impossible, but he would not give up, and with a clever breeding program carried out in the field, he succeeded. There are now more than two-hundred and forty black robins, living on four different islands.

But all of our efforts will be in vain and there will be no point in expending energy and money to save species, create parks and reserves, if we do not raise new generations of young people to be better stewards of Earth and its wild places. This is why I now travel the world three hundred days a year - to develop our JGI Roots & Shoots for youth. It is a symbolic name: roots creep underground everywhere and make a firm foundation; shoots seem new and small, but to reach the light can break apart brick walls - brick walls of over-population, soil erosion, desertification, poverty, disease, over consumption, pollution, global warming, cruelty, crime and warfare. Hundreds and thousands of roots and shoots - young people - around the world can break through and save the world. They can heal so many of the hurts that we have inflicted on Earth - partly through selfishness and materialistic lifestyles, but also through ignorance and a lack of understanding of the overall picture, the interconnectedness of all life.

Roots & Shoots began in Tanzania in 1991 and there are now some five-thousand active groups in more than sixty countries. These groups, from kindergarten to university, are involved in three kinds of hands-on projects that demonstrate care and concern for the environment, for non-human animals, and for the local community. They share their own problems and what they are doing to try to help with other Roots & Shoots groups in other neighborhoods, other countries. Inspiring young people, giving them hope, is my contribution to the future. For without hope people sink into apathy - what is the use of even trying to save something if you believe that it is all too late, that we have harmed the planet to the point of no return? It is not too late - there are still wilderness areas and dedicated and passionate people working to protect them, polluted land and water can be purified, man-made deserts can bloom again, animal and plant species on the brink of extinction given another chance. Attitudes towards animals and nature are changing. People are tiring of the materialistic consumer unsustainable lifestyles as they seek for meaning in their lives. We are beginning to realize that until crippling poverty is alleviated there can be no peace. And until we learn to live in peace with nature there will be no peace between men. To bring about these changes, to save life on Earth as we know it, we must ALL get into the act. We must all, we who truly care, do our bit to make the world a better place. We each have different contributions to make, in different fields, but we each have a role to play. It is our individual efforts, around the planet, that will make the difference.

This glorious book brings the beauty, the grace, the vitality of one of the most beautiful of animals right into the living room. Look into the eyes of these cheetahs, each one with his or her own personality and life force, and let them speak to your heart. Howard has written 'The cheetah is the fastest animal on earth, but it cannot outrun man' - meaning, of course, that it cannot escape man's destruction of its habitat, man's cruelty, man's indifference. But with your help the cheetah can be saved. They need your help desperately, and they need it now. Let us make a commitment to the cheetah and to future generations of our children: 'We will not allow this glorious creature to vanish before our very eyes'. And then the cheetah will run, fastest of them all, into the future.

Jane Goodall

Founder - the Jane Goodall Institute
UN Messenger of Peace

Dr. Jane Goodall began her landmark study of chimpanzees in Tanzania in 1960 under the mentorship of anthropologist and paleontologist Dr. Louis Leakey. Her work at the Gombe National Park has become the foundation of future primatological research and redefines the relationship between humans and animals.

Dr. Goodall's work is one of the longest uninterrupted wildlife studies in existence. In 1977, she established the Jane Goodall Institute, which supports a broad range of research, education and conservation programs. Dr. Goodall travels over three-hundred days a year speaking about the threats to chimpanzees and the difficulties facing wildlife and conservation.

Dr. Goodall has received numerous honors including the Medal of Tanzania, The National Geographic Society's Hubbard Medal, Japan's prestigious Kyoto Prize and in 2001 she received the third Gandhi / King Award for Nonviolence, presented at the United Nations. She is the author of numerous publications and in April 2002, United Nations Secretary General Kofi Annan appointed Dr. Goodall as United Nations 'Messenger of Peace'.

INTRODUCTION

HOWARD G. BUFFETT

As a teenager in 1974, I stepped onto South African soil for the first time. I could not have imagined that almost thirty years later I would consider some of my best friends to be from this country. Also I could not have anticipated the passion I would develop for one of the world's most graceful cats, the cheetah. My passion was fueled by a special friendship that has developed over the past six years with Ann van Dyk, founder of The De Wildt Cheetah and Wildlife Centre.

In the past, I have published books and articles about the loss of our biodiversity, the continuing human encroachment on critical habitat needed for species survival, and our behavior that constantly forces animals toward extinction. Few people have done as much to fight this trend as Ann. Focused primarily on the cheetah, but never passing up an opportunity to help save other species, Ann has done more than any individual in the fight to save the cheetah population in Southern Africa. Thirty years ago when the cheetah seemed headed toward extinction, she founded De Wildt. Through unusual determination and commitment, Ann turned De Wildt into the pre-eminent cheetah-breeding and research center, at present the only approved CITES cheetah-breeding center in the world.

De Wildt cannot do it alone. Cheetahs, along with many other species, are being persecuted worldwide as human population growth increases consumption of resources and space. This continual pressure on the earth's assets creates new challenges for many animals, especially predators and primates. Like proverbial spots before your eyes, one minute a species is here, the next minute it is gone forever.

While species have come and gone through the millennia, in the past few decades human behavior has accelerated the threat to record levels. To correct this course, we must change our priorities and our focus. Conservation cannot be a fad; it must be an enduring philosophy diligently executed on a global basis.

In the following pages, through the lens of our cameras, Ann and I share with you some of the passion we have for Africa, especially for its cheetahs. We hope that future generations will have the same opportunity to view this wonderful animal. The survival of the cheetah and the habitat required for a sustainable future has become the responsibility of our generation. If we fail in this mission, few other achievements will matter in the long run, for without preserving nature, we destroy our future.

It is estimated that the cheetah originated over five million years ago, long before many of the other big cats.

1

THE SPOTTED CAT

Cheetahs are an ancient species, first noted in the Pliocene Era (between five and two million years ago). A carnivore (meat-eater), the mammal belongs to the cat family (Felidae). Its genus is *Acynonyx* and one species, *jubatus,* is found primarily in Africa. Historically, this species ranged throughout areas of Africa, the Arabian Peninsula, Asia Minor and India. However, there is evidence that *A. pardinensis* roamed Europe and that two cheetah-like species, *Miracinonyx inexpectatus* and *Miracinonyx trumani* were residents of North America millions of years ago. Fossil remains indicate some variations in physical traits, but it is generally accepted that *A. pardinensis* represented the earlier versions of today's cheetahs.

Today isolated areas with cheetahs are found in North Africa and Asia (notably Iran). Populations are diminishing rapidly, and the cheetah's main habitat is primarily confined to two strips, one belt running just north of equatorial Africa and the other reaching down through Eastern Africa to Southern Africa. The word 'cheetah' has been adopted from the Hindi word 'chita' which means 'spotted one', this being an indication of the feline's earlier habitation in Asia. To the ancient Egyptians, cheetahs were revered. Many tombs of kings show the cats featured in funerary adornments.

In Southern Africa, cheetahs (and other felines) are barely represented in San rock art, possibly because the animals were of no use to the society that produced the images. Ceremonially, however, spotted pelts have long been favored by indigenous populations throughout sub-Saharan Africa and the practice continues in some areas today. The Western world's furrier trade in spotted and other animal pelts was finally considered unacceptable in the late twentieth century, thus putting an end to what most consider a tasteless whim of fashion.

Prior to extinction of the cheetah in India, captive cheetahs were used to hunt game. Similar to the way falcons have been trained to hunt and kill prey and then return obediently to their handlers, cheetahs were taught the same. Above right, a handler prepares a cheetah for a chase by removing his blindfold. Below right, a cheetah has made a successful kill and is rewarded with a cup of blood from the animal. (Photographs, 1940, Gujarat, India).

Photograph courtesy of John and Frank Craighead

Photograph courtesy of John and Frank Craighead

The facial tear line is unique to the cheetah; it is one of the most distinguishing characteristics among large African cats.

The leopard is a much more powerful cat than the cheetah. The average leopard may weigh as much as the largest of male cheetahs, approximately sixty-four kilograms (one-hundred forty pounds).

A visual difference between the two cats is their coat pattern: spots of leopards are formed as rosettes (above); cheetahs have solid separated spots, oval or round in shape (opposite, top right).

Some adult cheetahs have a short ruff, possibly left from its days as a young cub when it sported a large, light-colored mantle.

Physically, cheetahs have three strong distinguishing features: spots, facial tear lines (dark lines which extend from the eye, a short way down the nose and then outward down to the mouth) and a thin, graceful body. It is believed the purpose of the tear line is a combination of glare-reduction and an enhancement of the animal's vicious posing when snarling - a form of war paint. The spots of a cheetah are true spots, not rosettes like those of a leopard, and vary in size from small flecks on the face to three centimeters (a little over an inch) in diameter on the back of the pelt.

As a species, the cheetah is not aggressive, preferring to back off in the face of attack. They are thus constantly open to predation by larger carnivores such as lions. On the other hand, because of their passive nature, both wild and captive-born cheetahs have earned the reputation of cats with gentle personalities. If one has ever had the privilege of getting to know a cheetah intimately, one will know how true this is. In past times, this gentle nature has made it possible for cheetahs to be trained by man for use in hunting. This was more common in eastern countries such as India, but occasionally it occurred in Africa.

In contrast to the leopard, the cheetah's teeth are smaller, allowing for larger nasal passages to facilitate air intake during high-speed chases. The cheetah's muzzle is flatter, the ears are set back, and its eyes are large, well-spaced, and designed for good bifocal vision. All of these features provide advantages for speed.

The leopard's physique is better suited for climbing, stealth, stalking and pouncing.

Young cheetahs are playful and often demonstrate mock hunting by stalking, chasing, pouncing and interacting with siblings.

As the sun sets and optimum visibility is reduced, it becomes less likely that this cheetah will hunt for food.

Rarely do cheetahs move about at night since they are diurnal, resting at night and active during the day. In daylight hours, however, activity is usually confined to the cooler periods - the start and end of the day. Instinctively the large cat knows how to conserve energy and how to keep cool when out on the hot African plains.

Just before sunrise, this cheetah missed an attempt to take an impala. As the sun rises, the steam from the cheetah's increased body heat is visibly expended in the cool morning air.

From a termite mound in the Okavango Delta (Botswana) a cheetah scans the surrounding area. After spotting a herd of impala, the cat descends to thick grass for cover and a short time later, it makes a successful kill.

This animal demonstrates typical cheetah behavior by using a fallen tree branch to gain a better view of the landscape.

Like most cats, cheetahs do climb. They cannot match the agility of leopards in high boughs, but it is not uncommon to see cheetahs of all ages on the lower branches of sturdy trees. Similarly, from time to time they will leap onto any tall object in the landscape, such as a rock or mound of earth. This may be a game-spotting technique, particularly on a flat landscape.

Cheetahs have often been described as having non-retractable claws like dogs, but this is not accurate. Their claws have no sheaths, so they appear to remain protracted; however, they can be withdrawn to a small degree. Claws of cheetahs play an important role in prey capture and self defense, particularly the dew claws of the front legs.

The tail of the cheetah is long and prominent, and when in flight it acts as a steering rudder or system of balance. Fur is usually short, though animals kept in zoos where climates reach below-zero temperatures in winter will develop thicker, more bushy coats.

Born without teeth, cubs will develop twenty-six. At maturity an adult cheetah has thirty teeth, sixteen in the upper jaw and fourteen in the lower. Milk teeth are lost at the age of about eight months.

Male cheetahs, in general, are larger than females, but this can vary from litter to litter.

From a static position, cheetahs have been known to accelerate to seventy-two kph (forty-five mph) in only two seconds - an amazing burst of speed.

As the sun begins to sink toward the horizon, cheetahs will take advantage of the cooler temperatures to move about, mark territory and possibly hunt before dark.

In the wild, cheetahs often use mounds for spotting game. However, it has been observed that they also use them frequently in captivity if they are available. Some believe cheetahs that have access to mounds in captive conditions demonstrate less stress.

Approximately ten thousand years ago at the end of the last ice age, a large number of mammals became extinct. The cheetah species was also nearly extinguished. Subsequent population bottlenecks reduced the cheetah population even further to an estimated one hundred thousand in 1900. It is likely that less than fifteen thousand exist today.

2

ENDANGERED OR NOT

Like proverbial spots before your eyes, cheetahs are here one moment and gone the next. That is because the animal is reputedly the fastest creature on earth, reaching speeds of up to one hundred fourteen kph (seventy mph). If you're fortunate enough to witness these animals in the wild, it will be a memorable experience.

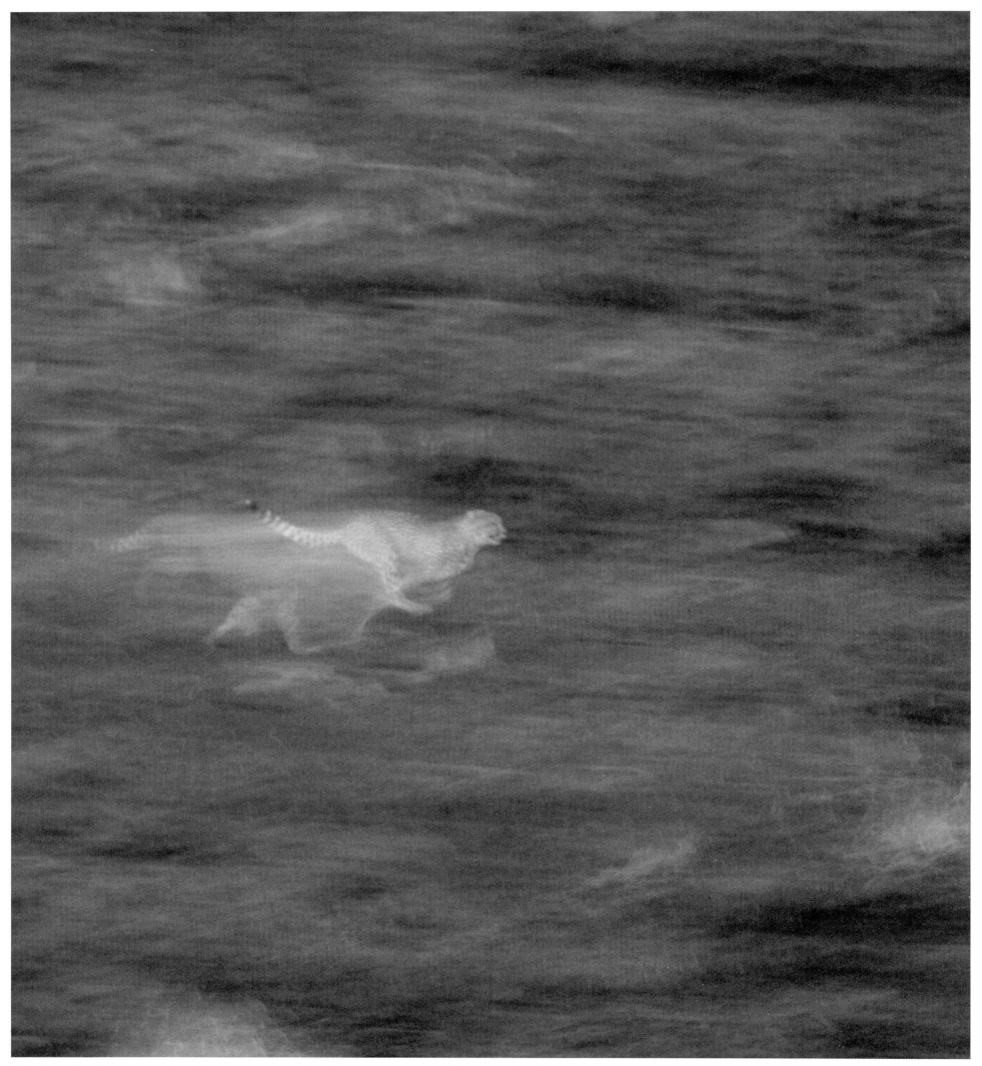

The length of a cheetah's stride at top speed is about nine meters (almost thirty feet).

Like every animal species, cheetahs are vulnerable to extinction, and at this moment in our planet's history, like so many other species, they have never been more threatened.

The reasons for this threat are twofold: cheetahs require an exceptionally large habitat and today their traditional home is being dominated and swiftly diminished by *Homo sapiens.* Two viewpoints about this alarming fact prevail. One is a 'let-nature-take-its-course' view that believes in the survival of the fittest without man's intervention. The other outlook searches for every solution imaginable in an effort to try and reverse the state of affairs.

In the past, there has been controversy about the validity of cheetahs being endangered. Counting them in the wild is extremely difficult because the species is nomadic, making accurate data hard to compile. It is nevertheless accepted internationally that the species is indeed endangered. Due to the species' relatively short lifespan (about ten to twelve years in the wild, fifteen years in captivity) and ever-diminishing habitat, trade in cheetahs and their skins is prohibited by CITES (the Convention on International Trade in Endangered Species).

A coalition of four sedated male cheetahs is relocated to a new wildlife reserve. Finding suitable habitat for cheetahs remains a formidable challenge. As humans continue to expand land uses, cheetahs increasingly risk confrontation with landowners.

In terms of general habitat, today's wild cheetahs are confined to sub-Saharan African grasslands which are settled and cultivated by humans. Apart from these isolated farming areas where cheetahs still roam free, the habitat of this animal is artificially controlled, such as in wildlife parks or game reserves. Ironically, these areas are administered by man, the very same super-abundant species which threatens the livelihood of so much flora and fauna today.

Specific habitat is important for cheetahs. Good cover must be available for hunting, sufficient prey must be sustained by the vegetation and protective growth must be present for cubs.

Today's cheetah species once roamed North Africa, India and sub-Saharan Africa. The species was extinct in India by the early 1950s, and today in Northern Africa and Asia only small isolated areas support cheetahs. The most likely places to see wild cheetah today are Botswana, Kenya, Namibia, South Africa, Tanzania, Zambia and Zimbabwe.

Although cheetahs are regularly found on the plains of East Africa, the species also flourishes in bushveld savanna where good visibility and a variety of cover contribute to higher success with hunting and cub survival.

Cheetahs adapt to a wide variety of habitat. Open areas where the cheetah can utilize its speed, combined with good cover and opportunities to gain elevation, provide an ideal environment.

On the plains of Eastern Africa, cheetahs are able to gain a good view of the landscape. This, however, can also work against the cat, allowing both prey and other predators to more easily spot the cheetah.

Males often stay with male siblings or bond with unrelated males to form life-long coalitions.

3

SOCIETY OF SPOTS

Traditionally cheetahs have been regarded as solitary cats. However, they are frequently seen in groups - a mother with young or a coalition of male adults. The latter usually originates from male littermates remaining together in adulthood. The females of that litter separate from the group and become solitary.

A mother with cubs is a self-contained unit that keeps to itself, perpetuating the idea of the solitary character of the species. When her offspring reach an age of about two years, the mother leaves them to fend for themselves. That mother is now re-eligible to mate. By chance, if subsequent litters meet earlier offspring, the youngsters will show no sign of family recognition.

Females are solitary animals except when they are raising their cubs.

Mothers generally take good care of their young, providing protection and affection.

A mother will nurse her cubs for the first three to four months. Lactating females require twice as much food as they normally would and therefore must hunt more frequently. Cubs remain dependent upon their mother for about eighteen months.

Male cubs are likely to form relationships which keep them together for life. After independence, a female may stay with other siblings for a short time; however, she will eventually break away to lead a solitary existence. This system of social males and solitary females is unique among cat species.

Litters vary in size, the average being three or four cubs, although up to eight have been recorded. Large litters probably correspond with the high mortality rate of cheetah cubs and are a compensatory factor. Numbers vary in different areas, but in the wild, cub mortality is extremely high, particularly for cubs less than six months of age. In the South African lowveld, cub mortality is estimated as high as seventy percent and in the Serengeti (Tanzania) as high as eighty percent.

The animals are excellent communicators. A male marks its territory by squirting urine onto tall objects such as trees. The typical stance of squirting is with tail upright and back towards the tall object. 'Marking' designates territory, and this is respected if the urine is freshly sprayed. Territories can overlap from time to time, simply because areas would be too large to mark on a regular basis.

Cheetahs make a full range of cat noises: mews, meows, hisses, growls and purrs, as well as the high-pitched birdlike 'chirp' and 'chirr'. Hisses are usually accompanied by spitting and growling and a raising of the front paws simultaneously followed by a sharp stamping of the ground. This latter behavior is intended to frighten off a possible predator or enemy.

Territorial male cheetahs scent-mark their ranges extensively, far more than nomadic males. The latter generally do not remain in one place for more than a few days and will cover vast areas. Thus they are often in poorer physical condition than their territorial counterparts or males belonging to a coalition.

After becoming separated during a hunt, this male cheetah calls its companion.

Like most cats, cheetahs spend a fair amount of time resting. In hot weather, they can spend up to ninety percent of their time lying in the shade.

After a meal, cheetahs often groom one another by licking. They demonstrate this behavior within family groups in what appears to be a sign of affection. This behavior may also advance bonding between members of coalitions.

A cheetah on the Serengeti plains uses a technique sometimes employed when concealment is not a viable option. It casually approaches the group of animals. The trigger point for the chase will be when one of the animals takes flight. This cheetah will focus on an animal that it is capable of bringing down - not likely one of the adult zebras in the background.

Cheetahs are not adept at defending themselves. Built for speed, not confrontation, they use several methods to try and intimidate potential attackers. Their most aggressive behavior is a lunge forward with the front legs hitting the ground simultaneously accompanied by hissing, spitting, growling and a show of teeth. Although this can be convincing, there is little to back it up, and cheetahs will quickly retreat before risking injury to themselves.

Photograph courtesy of Thomas D. Mangelsen

These two adult males have approached a female with four male sub-adult cubs. The female tries to fend off the two males in an effort to protect her offspring. One theory is that if the males kill or drive off the cubs, the female will come into estrus.

Later, the female and her four sub-adult cubs take shelter alongside stationary vehicles as the two males continue to harass them. Eventually the males move off, leaving the female and her offspring unharmed. However, other cases record conflicts so violent that some have resulted in cheetah deaths.

Cheetah aggression can appear to be quite intimidating - ears back, nose wrinkled and teeth showing. However, cheetahs are not likely to engage in this behavior unless provoked or threatened.

A cheetah is unlike other wild cats in that once tamed, usually it will not revert back to a state of wildness. When meeting a human, a deep-throated purr is generally the first indication of a tamed animal, and like domestic cats, lasting recognition and deep affectionate bonds can develop between tamed cheetahs and humans.

Cheetahs display typical cat gestures, such as licking, head rubbing, front feet stamping accompanied by growling and hissing (aggression), head ducking and snarling (aggression). The most common characteristic is the casual aloofness that all cats possess.

Cheetahs can develop strong bonds with humans.

Head rubbing is common most often in litters, but also among coalition members.

This magnificent pelt is a rare occurrence in the wild.

4

THE KING CHEETAH

The coat of the king cheetah is not a representation of a separate species or subspecies, but is merely a variation in coloring. The normal-spotted coat consists of dark spots evenly spread over beige to white background. Dark beige fur is on the back, white on the belly. Several dark rings occur at the end of the tail, the tip being white and bushy.

This is an example of the normal-spotted coat, by far the most commonly encountered.

Prior to the research conducted at De Wildt, there was widespread speculation as to the classification of the king cheetah (above). Some considered it a subspecies, while others viewed it as a hybrid between leopard and cheetah. It may have been a king cheetah at the root of a legendary Zimbabwean cat which was said to be neither lion, leopard nor cheetah.

The king variety of cheetah is the result of a recessive gene, similar in origin to other animals such as the 'spirit bear', a white or pale colored black bear found in Canada, and the 'black panther', an all black jaguar which still bears its typical rosette spots found in Central and South America. There is one reliable report of an all-black cheetah sighted in 1925 in Kenya.

In the case of the king cheetah, the face markings are similar to those of the normal-spotted cheetah, but the cheeks and forehead are darkly mottled. The beige to white background of the king cheetah is marked with black lozenge-shaped patterns which form long stripes down the length of the back. It is an exceptionally handsome pelt and one can understand why this specimen was hunted in preference to its more common spotted relative.

Each king cheetah has a unique and recognizable coat pattern, as individual as the human fingerprint.

A king and a normal-spotted cub may be born in the same litter, provided the mother is carrying the gene for the king coat.

Although to the human eye a king cheetah's coat provides excellent camouflage, it has yet to be ascertained whether the coat is actually an advantage or disadvantage during hunting or when eluding predators. Sightings of kings in the wild are extremely rare, leading to speculation that the coat may be a disadvantage. However, low numbers may be due to the paucity of king gene carriers or even to a high percentage of animals being killed for their unique coats.

At about ten days, cubs will begin to open their eyes and their milk teeth will also start to grow. The cubs above are twelve days old.

In 1981, the first king cheetah to be born in captivity was at The De Wildt Cheetah Centre, near Pretoria, South Africa. Since then more than sixty king cheetahs have been born at the Centre as part of an ongoing endangered wildlife program. Because records of each king-gene carrier are meticulously kept, profiles can be built enabling wildlife researchers to understand and observe implications of small gene pools amongst wild animals.

Recessive genes must be present in both parents to produce a king offspring.

Unlike the genetic coat variation of the king, coats of cheetahs can occasionally vary based on environmental factors. Cheetahs living in the Sahara Desert region tend to be paler in color and it is logical to assume that over time these animals have adapted to their environment in order to survive. It is common in other animals for variations of coat color, animal size or length of fur to occur, thus providing better camouflage or protection in their surroundings.

A cheetah family develops strong bonds between mother and cub and between siblings.

5

MOTHER AND CUB

An adult female is old enough to bear a litter at the age of about two years. Cheetahs do not have a particular season for cycling, and a mother is capable of coming into season immediately after losing a litter of cubs - an event which frequently occurs in the wild. Normally, however, a female will only come into estrus again once her cubs are full grown - about two years.

Mothers take full responsibility for raising cubs since fathers are absent and play no part.

Cubs are completely dependent upon their mother from the time they are born until they separate. At about seven to eight months, offspring will begin to take part in hunting, yet they are not able to survive unaided during this training period and rely on their mother's hunting to sustain them.

The fact that she is in estrus is signalled to males through excreted hormones. Once a male has been accepted by the female, a process of mounting, playing, being repelled and acceptance follows - all of which can last a few days. Thereafter the male will disappear, playing no role whatsoever in the care and upkeep of his offspring. Pregnancy lasts from ninety to ninety-five days.

Cubs are playful and unaware of what the future holds for them. The vast majority of cheetah cubs born in the wild do not survive. The chances of reaching maturity increase slightly if the young live in areas where there are lower numbers of competing predators - especially lions.

After selecting a suitably protected place, usually in long grass, the female gives birth alone. She eats the placenta and breaks the membranes of each cub with her teeth. Of its own accord, the umbilical cord falls off the cub within a few days.

Like domestic cats, the young are born blind. They weigh approximately three hundred grams (ten and a half ounces) and their coloring is noticeably different from that of adults. Spots and other markings are not well demarcated. The lower body is covered with very dark fur and the upper body with a pale, buff-to-grey-colored mantle of long fur. The long fur is similar in color and texture to the vegetation in which the mother will leave her young when she is out hunting for food, and possibly the purpose of the hair is to act as camouflage.

A newborn cheetah gives no indication of its future long-legged and graceful form, for it is no more than a chubby ball of fur. Because its ears are small in relation to its head, it resembles a round-faced teddy bear.

Young cheetah cubs are defenseless and vulnerable. Their mother will move them frequently, hiding them in thick grass, heavy thickets or in gullies with dense vegetation.

By the time the cubs are full grown the mantle will have disappeared, although vestiges of long fur may remain on the neck and shoulder area.

The female cheetah must by nature be a strong and capable mother, for in her society no nursemaid or family support exists. After giving birth, the lactating mother must feed her cubs, defend them from predators and also procure her own food. Probably as a security measure, a mother moves her young every few days to a new lair. She holds a cub in her mouth by the scruff of its neck, carrying the litter one by one. Mothers are very protective of their young at all times and will be unusually aggressive if approached when the litter is new-born.

After ten or twelve days the eyes of the cubs open. In the beginning the iris is very dark in color, but it turns to golden brown within weeks. Cubs are suckled for about five or six weeks and are then offered meat by the mother. After three weeks the cubs begin to try to walk, and by six weeks the youngsters are ready for their first outing with their mother. At this early stage, they are still on shaky legs and mother has to make frequent 'chirrp' and 'chirr' calls to urge them on.

Abundance and variety of food enhances cheetah cub survival. Cheetah births are not seasonal, and it has been observed in some areas that conception is more frequent when high levels of prey are available.

East African cubs born during the rainy season are more likely to reach maturity than those born in dry months when fires sweep through the plains.

Mother and cubs form a close-knit unit and there is ample time for play, licking and caressing. At times when the playful cubs become too boisterous, a tired mother is often seen disciplining the young with a swift cuff of her paw. Most times, looking like a sphinx, she stoically stares into the distance while the cubs clamber over her. Licking one another is also a form of communication and is done frequently, on occasion the mother's large round tongue nearly knocking a youngster off its feet.

By the time the cubs are about three months old they are able to share the mother's kill. During the kill itself they will remain out of sight, only appearing in response to their mother's calls, a signal that all is safe. At this stage of development, the cub's long sandy-colored ruff of neck hair is still visible but sparse, and the coat markings gain definition. Long legs are developing and fat bellies are receding.

Playful antics will develop the necessary skills for hunting and protection.

Cheetah cubs will spend many hours of the day interacting.

After wrestling and chasing, cubs are likely to show mutual affection for one another.

This frisky cub is trying to get its mother's attention, but the mother is more interested in finding a suitable meal.

Chasing, fleeing and tripping one another, these cubs begin to learn how to use their bodies and keep their balance.

Hunting is taught to the young by the mother in a gradual process. In the early stages, a mother often brings a small kill to her cubs who are not yet capable of bringing down an animal on their own. But as cubs' prowess develops, so do their bodies. In time, after about two years, they are no longer cubs - they are adults.

The mother will break away from her cubs at about eighteen to twenty months. The littermates stay together as a unit for awhile, after which the females will leave the males, as each female seeks out her own territory. Males frequently remain together as a coalition.

Cheetahs are polyestrous and can therefore give birth to cubs at any time of year. Should a female lose her cubs, she may come into estrus within a few weeks.

When a female cheetah breaks away from her cubs, it is usually an abrupt separation, slipping away at a moment when the cubs are unaware of her departure. A female cheetah leads a difficult life, being solitary by nature and raising cubs with no support system.

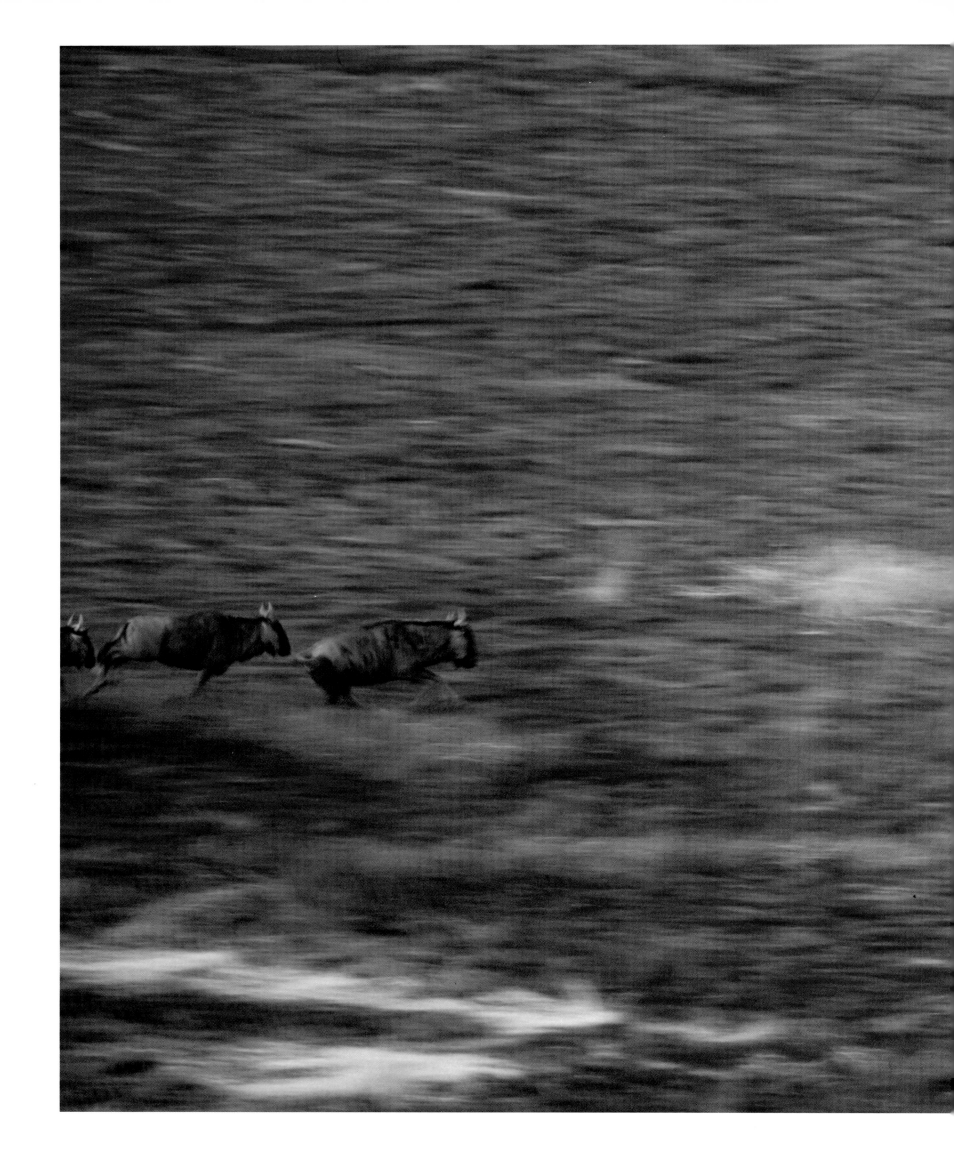

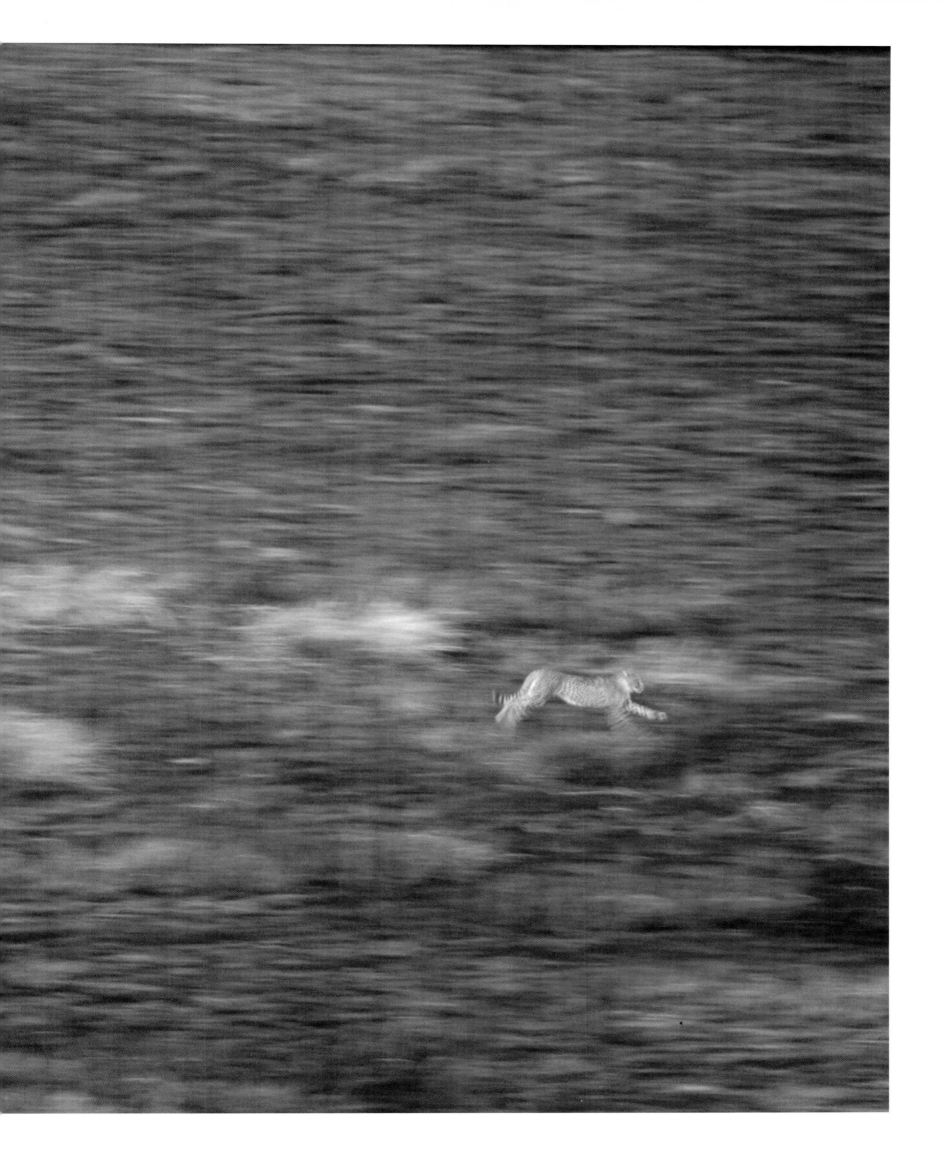

A coalition of males will have more success defending territory and hunting than will a solitary male.
Preceding pages: After chasing a herd of wildebeest, the larger animals turn on the cheetah.

6

THE HUNTER

Known as an efficient hunter, a cheetah has speed on its side and will kill only when hungry or to feed young (in the case of females). Acceleration, as opposed to sustained speed, is the cheetah's main asset. In a mere two to three seconds, and often from a static position, it can reach a speed of up to one hundred fourteen kph (seventy mph). A cheetah cannot maintain a chase for any length of time. The essence of its hunting technique is the high-speed spurt and the element of surprise.

Twice during a cheetah's stride, all four feet are airborne, once when the body is fully extended and again when all its feet are tucked under its body.

The cheetah must react to each move as its prey is fleeing. With eyes narrowed against the dust kicked up from the animal being chased, the cheetah must remain focused. From the start, the cheetah will target only one animal and during the chase it may pass other suitable animals standing on the 'sidelines'. The cheetah's top speed can only be maintained for about two hundred fifty to three hundred meters (seven hundred fifty to nine hundred feet). If prey is not caught within three hundred meters, the cheetah will likely abort the hunt in an effort to conserve energy and to avoid overheating.

'Speed' and 'cheetahs' are analogous. Hard foot pads and strong claws provide traction, big nasal cavities and lungs provide excellent oxygen intake and a large heart and adrenal glands allow for rapid physical reaction. Streamlined bones, a flexible spine and a tail that is used as a rudder are all advantageous for speed.

A cub will quickly learn hunting techniques, such as stalking, from its mother. Siblings stalk and pounce on each other to develop these hunting skills. While prowling, in order not to alert prey to their presence, adult cheetahs will sometimes freeze their positions for extended periods.

The ability to attain high speed is due to the unique skeletal and muscular makeup of the animal: a combination of long slender legs, a supple spine, separated back muscles that act together forcefully, muscles attached to the scapula horizontally and a supple rotation of hips. It is an unusual and unique combination of muscular and skeletal evolution. With this natural elegance and well proportioned body, it is an extraordinary creature.

Keen eyesight aids in the initial selection of prey, which, after being identified as a likely kill, is stalked and chased at high speed so that it is short of breath and passive by the time it is first tripped by its captor. The animal may still put up a fight, but if the cheetah proves to be the stronger combatant, death will follow swiftly - by suffocation or as the result of a bite to the throat or head area causing central nervous system damage. Struggling prey may be contained successfully by the cheetah's strong dewclaws which act as hooks.

Unlike heavier cats, such as lions or leopards, cheetahs do not need muscular strength to subdue their prey: speed is their asset. Stalking can take up to half an hour and sometimes prey is not stalked at all. A moving animal is always selected over a stationary one.

Towards the end of a chase, cheetahs use their sharp dewclaws to hook prey, throwing it off balance or slowing it down. Another favorite technique is to trip the prey with a forefoot, knocking its hind leg out from under it.

Like lions, cheetahs may resort to clan or team hunting as a technique. There have been instances recorded where mothers with near-adult cubs have hunted in unison, as well as groups of males together in coalitions.

As one cheetah keeps a wary eye out for intruders, the others will continue to eat. It is not unusual for cheetahs to share this sentry duty.

With the possibility of losing their catch, cheetahs normally eat as much as they can in as little time as possible. This cheetah has just gorged itself on a kill.

Keeping a keen watch for unwanted company, this cheetah finishes off a blesbok, leaving the head. Normally only the soft flesh of an animal is consumed.

Having had its initial fill, this cheetah is alert and cautious of possible interruption by other predators or scavengers. After eating all it can, the cat will go for three to four days before making another kill. For optimal physical condition, cheetahs require about three to four kilograms (about seven to eight pounds) of meat per day and can consume up to fourteen kilograms (thirty pounds) at one time.

Once prey has been killed, it is dragged to the shade of a shrub or tree so that the heavily panting captor can recover its breath and be afforded some measure of protection. Even if no shrubbery is available, instinctively cheetahs will move their prey to another location before beginning to eat. Hindquarters of the prey will be the first part to be tackled, then the fleshier parts of the abdomen, while the bowels, head and legs are almost never eaten.

A cub repeatedly investigates a nyala which has been killed by its mother - possibly the cub's first taste of flesh.

The final breath of this impala has not yet been taken. The cheetah will keep a vise-like grip on the windpipe until this animal is lifeless. It can take several minutes to suffocate the animal. The cheetah will likely drag the carcass under a tree or bush, seeking both shade and cover from other animals.

A mother drags an impala over four kilometers (two and a half miles), mostly uphill, to the place she has left her four cubs. When her cubs are within sight, she is confronted by a hyena and has no alternative but to relinquish the impala and move her cubs to safety.

Usually cheetahs will select smaller prey, such as young antelope or hares, and a variety of other animals depending on availability. The younger the cheetah, or the older and more infirm, the smaller its prey tends to be. On average fourteen kilograms (thirty pounds) of meat is eaten when a kill is made, and then for the next two to five days no food will be required. In captivity, adults are provided with between three and four kilograms (about seven or eight pounds) of meat on a daily basis. If an animal has had its fill, it will leave the carcass, almost never to return to it. Cheetahs devour only freshly killed meat. Often a good deal of meat is left on a carcass, and as a cheetah leaves its kill, scavengers move in to clean it up - though at times scavengers actually deprive the cheetah of its own kill.

Ideal prey for a cheetah is an animal weighing about thirty kilograms (sixty-six pounds).
Impala, gazelle, duiker, bushbuck, steenbok and springbok are all top choices.

Other targets may ocassionally include the young of larger animals, possibly waterbuck, kudu, nyala, zebra or giraffe.
A coalition of several males will likely have more success capturing larger prey. Cheetahs hunt by stalking or ambushing,
but sometimes from a position of concealment, they take unsuspecting prey by surprise.

This cheetah pursues a gazelle at top speed in the Serengeti National Park (Tanzania).

On the heels of a gazelle, a split-second miscalculation in tripping the prey will leave this pursuing cheetah without a meal.

At one stage there was debate as to whether captive-born cheetahs would ever be able to catch prey on their own, since this was thought to be a mother-taught skill. However, it has been proven that instincts and all other attributes of the hunter surface in time of hunger or need, though some cheetahs may possess greater prowess as hunters than others.

After a long chase, this cheetah will not begin to eat for over thirty minutes since it must recover from exhaustion. A cheetah's breathing can increase tenfold during a chase.

With a full stomach, this cheetah lies within eyesight of her kill, yet distant enough for a quick retreat should another predator appear.

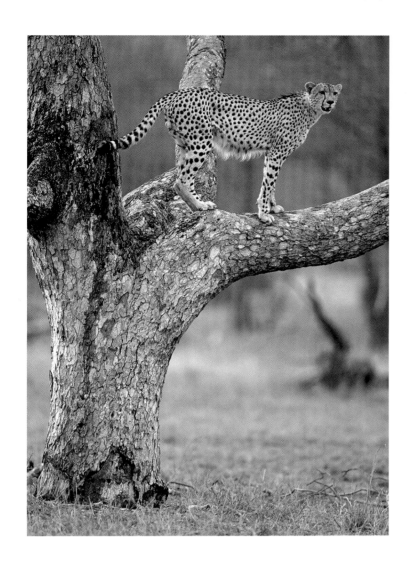

Cheetahs are not exceptionally good climbers. Paws of cheetahs are suited for fast running, and their hard foot pads make it difficult for them to climb. However, cheetahs of all ages will be seen on the large lower branches of trees.

Not being aggressive makes cheetahs vulnerable to attack by other predators. They are no match for lions when they happen to cross paths or invade their territory. It has been observed that cubs in a lair left unattended by a mother have been killed but not eaten by lions. In the wild, the mortality rate of cheetahs is high, a large number falling prey to lions, hyenas and leopards at some stage of life. Death also occurs from a variety of illnesses, including infectious feline enteritis ('cat flu'), kidney and liver disease, rabies, tuberculosis and other bronchial ailments, dysentery resulting from parasites such as ringworm, tapeworm, etc. And all too often wounds sustained from altercations with other animals or fellow cheetahs or even septic sores produced by porcupine quills, can result in a painful, lingering death.

Cubs jump onto accessible branches and climb frequently, both to test their ability and also to gain a better view of the landscape. This skill is important later when they hunt for themselves.

Speed and agility are important attributes for a hunter.

Cheetahs are well built to hunt both large and small prey. However, small game such as duiker will provide enough food for only a day or two, after which the cheetah will have to hunt again.

A lion cub approaches an adult male, in a rare and sometimes dangerous behavior. Male lions will often kill cubs, particularly if they are not their own offspring.

7

THE COMPETITORS

Speed is necessary for a cheetah to capture its prey, but at times it is also needed for escape. This occurs when larger prey turns on the cheetah or when there is an altercation with another predator.

The greatest threat to lions (other than humans) are other lions. Here, these lionesses retreat with their cubs as several male lions invade their territory.   The next morning, the three smallest cubs are no longer with the pride.

The lion pride provides companionship and support to its members. There are usually around four to eight females and three to four territorial males in a pride. Often the males are siblings from the same litter.

Even with the cheetah's speed, it falls to the bottom of the list when it comes to survival as a predator. The lion is larger, has the pride to help bring down its prey and has almost every advantage over the cheetah except speed (although lions can reach speeds of sixty kilometers or nearly forty miles per hour). Like the cheetah, the lion cannot sustain this speed for long periods. The power of the lion is unmatched by any other African predator.

Lion prides vary in number and the average consists of between fourteen and sixteen members. The animals have high rates of success with mating and the largest danger facing a lion cub is an adult male lion. Male lions sometimes see cubs as a threat and accordingly may kill their own cubs. This threat to lion cubs, however, is not as great as those threats faced by cheetah cubs who are prey to every other predator, including lions.

Lions have a high degree of mating success, and lion cubs have a much higher survival rate than cheetah cubs. It is estimated that in the wild between two-thirds and three-quarters of all lion cubs survive.

Cheetahs are not scavengers and will eat only fresh meat. However, lions are opportunists and here a pride of lions enters the third day of eating an elephant carcass. This elephant was injured in a fire and later died, providing an easy meal for the group.

Because of their strength, size and cooperative hunting techniques, lions can bring down much larger prey than cheetahs. This buffalo weighs approximately eight hundred kilograms (eighteen hundred pounds).

By day or night, a lion is an efficient hunter. Cool temperatures of the evening and the cover of darkness make night the most suitable time for hunting.

After descending the tree, the leopard slowly and quietly stalks the animal.

When in range, it pounces on the animal and uses a choke hold on the neck of its prey similar to the suffocation technique used by cheetahs. The advantage of elevation, stealth and the efficiency of exerting little unnecessary energy makes the leopard an effective hunter and competitor of the cheetah.

Unlike cheetahs, leopards are quite at home high in trees.

Leopards also possess significant advantages over cheetahs. Avid climbers, leopards are at ease in trees, using them for protection and for sighting potential prey. They are extremely strong and often pull their kills high into trees to keep lions, hyenas and other animals from taking them. Cheetahs will climb, but they are not built for the difficult and challenging obstacles which leopards handle with ease.

One theory is that cheetahs often hunt during the day in order to avoid other predators like lions and leopards, which tend to hunt in the cooler hours of the day or at night. Cheetahs also take advantage of the earlier part of the morning, but will continue to hunt throughout the day. Fierce competition for food and the high rate of cub mortality make the odds for cheetah survival extremely low.

Leopards are capable of long vertical climbs. Their physical build enables easy movement in trees, rocks and uneven terrain. Similar in physique to the North American mountain lions and the South American jaguars, they are solitary and elusive animals.

Leopards frequently carry their kills into trees, where they may feed for several days safe from scavengers and other predators.

Should a leopard leave its kill temporarily, sometimes another leopard may take the carcass.

Leopards have stronger canine teeth than cheetahs. When their habitat is destroyed or usurped, their superior strength and adaptation skills afford them a good chance of survival.

Wild dogs are highly intelligent and social animals. Packs vary in size and may normally number between six and twenty. With less than six in a group, hunting efficiency can be impaired.

A pack of wild dogs usually has one dominant breeding pair, although there can also be a subordinate breeding female. Once a year females give birth, their litters averaging ten to fourteen pups. Young pups are guarded at the den while other pack members hunt. The entire pack shares in the responsibility of raising the young.

Wild dogs, although not widely found in areas where cheetahs roam, will quickly chase a cheetah off a kill. African painted wolves, as they have been romantically called, hunt in packs and have an intricate social structure. They cover great distances and will take down animals of small to medium size. Lions and leopards, particularly if outnumbered, would not likely challenge a large pack. Wild dogs have a combination of speed and endurance, along with coloring that provides excellent camouflage. Their teamwork makes them very successful hunters.

Like king cheetahs, coat variations of wild dogs can also identify individuals. Populations of wild dogs have declined dramatically in recent years mainly due to deliberate eradication by humans.

A large pack of wild dogs is a formidable opponent to almost all other predators, except perhaps lions and hyenas.

Hyenas are a particular menace to cheetahs. Due to the passive nature of cheetahs, their kills are often easy to steal. A cheetah would risk serious injury or death if it tried to defend its kill or its cubs against even a single hyena.

Since cheetahs eat fast, move off the kill at the first sign of danger and rarely return to the kill, jackals are often assured of a meal from the remains of a cheetah kill.

Hyenas and jackals often compete for the carcass of a cheetah's kill. Neither scavenger will usually pass up an opportunity for a meal. Hyenas are far more aggressive than jackals, though a jackal can spoil a cheetah kill by making the cheetah nervous enough to abandon the carcass. The jackal can also attract other predators which may cause cheetahs to move off the carcass.

One of the more unique competitors for prey is the python which is able to swallow an adult impala whole.

Servals (left) and caracals (right) occasionally compete with cheetahs for small prey.

In addition to suffering pressure from other predators, cheetahs have been hunted by man for years. Originally, human predation was by indigenous people, and later by hunters for sport and fur trading. Now, more often than not, conflict occurs over space.

The primary threat to cheetahs is man, through habitat encroachment and indiscriminate killing. Illegal sport hunting also threatens the population.

Tens of thousands of hectares of the cheetah's original habitat have been converted to other uses by humans. In many areas this use is for livestock, where cheetahs may find a calf an easy meal. Farmers often resort to killing problem cheetahs.

Encroachment on habitat, over-utilization of resources and conversion of land for agricultural use, result in fewer areas where cheetahs can roam free.

8

A DAY AT DE WILDT

Our mission at De Wildt is: 'To conserve, breed and wherever possible, re-introduce indigenous endangered species back into their natural habitat. We further aim to educate South Africans, especially the younger generation, to recognize and appreciate the flora and fauna of their country and to value their natural heritage. We conduct veterinary research into wildlife diseases relating to the animals bred at the Centre and develop strategies for the conservation of free- roaming cheetahs.'

Cheetah births may be new hope for species

CHEETAH CUBS BORN IN CAPTIVITY

SAVING THE CHEETAH
ARTICLE: Pretoria News

Cheetah cubs are thriving
Pretoria Bureau

Baby boom at De Wildt

Cheating extinction with captive breeding

Cubs and kings have attracted widespread attention in the media: headlines are from The Pretoria News, The Star, Sunday Times, Rand Daily Mail, *Midlands Observer,* SA Digest *and* SA Panorama.

Blissful Ignorance...a king cheetah cub and littermates bask with their mum in the sun at De Wildt, unaware of the fact that they have made world history (The Pretoria News).

De Wildt King cheetah cubs make world history

King cheetah is treated royally

Pretoria's 'miracle birth'

This little fellow is one of a kind

Already by the mid 1960s, the cheetah was a threatened species in Southern Africa. In 1971, The De Wildt Cheetah and Wildlife Centre had been established in order to unravel the mysteries and difficulties of breeding these animals in captive conditions. Over three decades later, and with the birth of almost six hundred cheetah cubs and sixty king cheetahs, the Centre has developed techniques whereby the subcontinent's diminished captive population has improved significantly, giving hope for the future.

Veterinarian Henk Bertschinger researches wildlife diseases as part of his work at De Wildt.

Wildlife diseases have been known to cut populations significantly, almost overnight. And so the work goes on and other endangered and threatened species are bred at De Wildt, including African wild dogs, brown hyenas, servals, African black-footed and small-spotted cats and a variety of vulture species including the rare Egyptian vulture.

Newborn wild dogs suckle their ever alert mother.

The gestation period for cheetahs is between ninety-one and ninety-five days. This mother is due to give birth shortly and she stands in front of the new birth shelter in which her cubs will be born.

Pregnant mothers are kept apart in the nursery section where sheltered huts simulate the long grass of the habitat where wild cats would hide their cubs. If mothers prove to be poor feeders and abandon their young, those cubs are removed from them. These litters are hand-reared, and at first they are bottle-fed every three hours.

Assistant director Vanessa Bouwer handles young cubs removed from their mother who would not or could not feed them properly.

Daybreak at De Wildt sees a truck winding its way through the enclosures, loaded with food for the animals. In summer the sun has already risen and the animals eagerly await the small truck's arrival. Winter mornings on the highveld are much cooler, but food is no less attractive in the pale early morning light. Always on the menu are chicken and horsemeat for adults and commercial pet food for youngsters. At feeding time, enclosures are checked for no-shows, a sign of illness, injury, birthing or behavioral change, and the condition of all is noted - especially pregnant mothers, cubs and the elderly.

To these cubs it seems the food truck will never come.

A nature conservation student feeds her young charges.

Curator Alan Strachan distributes meat and chickens.

Marilyn Dean aids blind children in handling a cheetah for the first time.

De Wildt provides a number of educational opportunities, and one of the most unusual is the chance for these children to view a rare king cheetah.

Then it's the routine of conducting tours around the Centre (twice daily, four days a week), fixing fences and cleaning enclosures. For the animals, there is the application of anti-tick and fly lotions, deworming, and relocation from enclosure to enclosure when necessary.

Schoolchildren learn about spotted and striped cheetahs.

On a hot summer's day, this cub is fast asleep.

At noon, when the sun is at its hottest, the Centre is at its sleepiest. Spotted bodies seek out shady places and lie seemingly lifeless. Wild dogs are silent. Bird sounds predominate.

By late afternoon activity restarts, and particularly the youngsters are spurred to action. Games are the order of the day and there is much release of energy as high spurts of speed, tripping antics and chasing one another ensues. Depending on the pattern of feeding, some charges are fed in the evening, and these animals now impatiently urge the bearer of food to arrive, with a variety of throaty noises - purrs and chirrps from cheetahs and serval cats, loud piercing yelps from wild dogs.

Then its bedding down, checking that all are safe and sound and anticipating the next day at sunrise. As the sun sets, there is the low hoot of the owl and as darkness descends, the high-pitched shrieks of wild jackals are heard as they make their way down from the Magaliesberg behind The De Wildt Centre to scavenge meat that is left out for them.

At De Wildt, people are able to view an endangered species at close quarters.

Should one try to save a species that is destined for extinction anyway? Is the artificial sustaining of life ethical? We do believe that we should be striving to conserve those species probably destined for extinction in this eon. The preservation of their natural environments that allow for self-sustained existence is also critical.

In this we will persevere with the utmost sincerity, integrity, ingenuity and energy. Here at De Wildt we don't wish those spots to fade before our very eyes.

These three cubs still have their long light-colored manes or mantles.

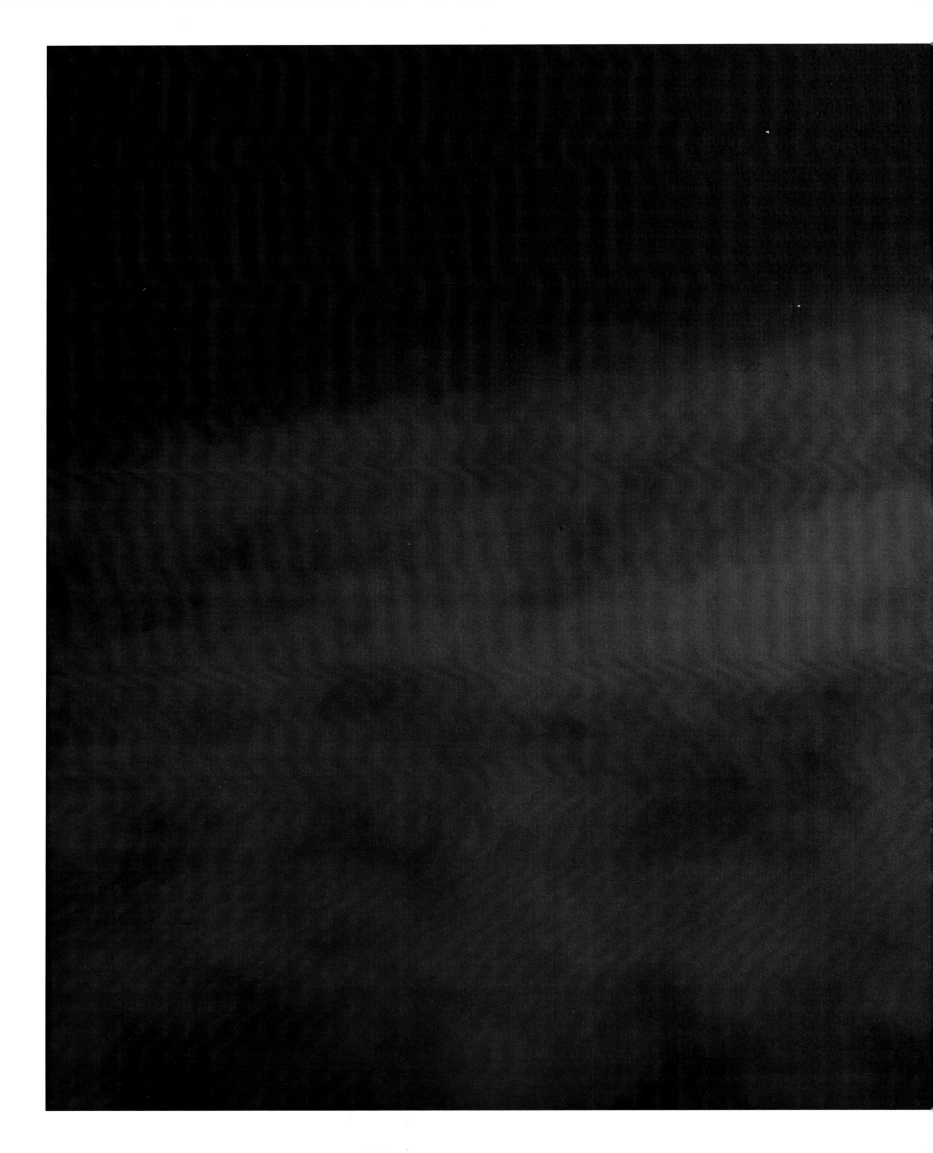

The night before this cheetah was to be released, a pride of lions approached the boma where he was housed. The cheetah became so agitated by the presence of the lions that in the commotion he broke his two front legs. He was transferred to The De Wildt Cheetah and Wildlife Centre for veterinary care and recovery. Unfortunately, after two years of care, he experienced complications from which he eventually died.

9

TOMORROW

The future of one of the world's oldest and most threatened cats hangs in the balance. Because every effort, regardless of scale, is important in the fight to ensure the survival of the cheetah, the Global Cheetah Forum (GCF) was formed in August of 2001. The group was organized by the Conservation Breeding Specialist Group and the North American Cheetah Species Survival Plan.

The GCF identified a number of priorities focusing on cheetah health, census data, survival of cheetahs in unprotected areas, linking *in situ* and *ex situ* cheetah conservation, and education and communication. Representatives from twelve countries participated in this landmark gathering, including Laurie Marker (Cheetah Conservation Fund/Namibia), Annie Beckhelling (Cheetah Outreach/South Africa), Dr. Sarah Durant (Serengeti Cheetah Project/Tanzania), Lisa Hanson (Africat/Namibia), Hoedspruit Endangered Wildlife Foundation (South Africa), Mokolodi Nature Reserve (Botswana), Marwell Zimbabwe Trust (Zimbabwe),and The De Wildt Cheetah and Wildlife Centre (South Africa).

Many of the participants of the Global Cheetah Forum have been leaders in cheetah conservation on a worldwide basis. Groundbreaking projects have been pursued by organizations such as the Cheetah Conservation Fund in Namibia, and by combining these innovative ideas with research from areas such as the Serengeti and lessons learned from successful breeding programs such as De Wildt, the GCF hopes to achieve a more comprehensive cheetah survival plan.

Founder of Cheetah Outreach, Annie Beckhelling, and handler, Dawn Glorer, show off Shadow to students at the Litha Primary School in Guguletu (outside Cape Town, South Africa). Educating Africa's young people about conservation will be critical to a successful future.

Hunter and hunted: an all-too-familiar scene today.

In South Africa, De Wildt continues to expand its role in cheetah conservation. De Wildt has provided valuable information for maintaining a viable captive cheetah population. Through its breeding program, De Wildt's cheetahs have been distributed worldwide, contributing to global knowledge of the species. This has included education, research and assistance with breeding procedures outside of South Africa. Unfortunately, these efforts will not be enough to sustain this animal's future.

Almost all existing wild cheetah populations are under increased pressure. In South Africa, De Wildt has emerged as a leader in resolving some of the resulting challenges. Sustaining wild cheetah populations and their required habitat involves complex issues. In almost all areas the underlying problem is the loss of land for cheetahs to roam freely. Over the years huge tracts of undeveloped land have been converted to cattle ranching and farming. Additional land has been converted to game farming for the purpose of hunting or breeding various species of antelope. This has further reduced the habitat available for free-roaming cheetahs. When 'problem' cheetahs are found on these game farms, the economic losses become even greater. This conversion of land has forced many predators into smaller areas with less available prey, therefore creating conflict with landowners. Because cheetahs require large areas for hunting, they are more adversely affected than most other predators. Also, the cheetah is often the scapegoat, mainly because it is a daytime hunter and is seen more frequently by farmers and ranchers. Hyenas, jackals, leopards and lions are more elusive and tend to hunt at night, avoiding contact with humans. Cheetahs also continue to be threatened by legal and illegal hunting.

The primary areas in South Africa with the largest remaining free-ranging cheetah populations are the Limpopo, North West and Northern Cape Provinces. Therefore, the majority of conflicts between cheetahs and farmers are encountered in these areas. Landowners frequently shoot 'problem' cheetahs to protect their economic interests. With a diminishing cheetah population, changes in land use that affect these animals, and landowners who often must protect their investment, the need for new and innovative solutions is now critical. The eradication of cheetahs in South Africa is a reality and a clear strategy is required to ensure that future generations will not lose this exquisite cat.

It seemed natural for De Wildt to address these challenges. De Wildt began by initiating a meeting involving all of the role players - game and livestock farmers, conservation authorities, non-governmental conservation bodies, academic institutions and other cheetah breeding centers. The outcome was the establishment of the National Cheetah Management Program (NCMP). The formation of the NCMP in 2000 was a bold step in dealing with the difficulties of 'problem' cheetahs that kill game and livestock on farms and ranches. The mission of the program is to ensure the long-term survival of the wild cheetah and protect its habitat through the implementation of a national management strategy. This approach must combine integrated conservation plans, research and education. It also required the establishment of a Cheetah Compensation Fund to provide the financial resources to compensate farmers for their losses and for capturing the cheetahs instead of killing them.

Farmers and conservationists come together to work on ways to prevent stock losses while ensuring survival of predatory cheetahs.

Under this governing body De Wildt formed its own working group in 2001, the Wild Cheetah Management Program (WCMP). Funding for this program comes both from De Wildt and overseas donors. Deon Cilliers, Chairman and Manager, and Kelly Wilson, Field Research Officer for WCMP, have met with more than 400 farmers in a dozen group encounters and hundreds of individual meetings. At the end of 2002 the program was successful in rescuing 47 cheetahs. The initial results are positive and demonstrate that this is a workable approach.

This cat has been successfully caught and will be released at a new location.

Deon Cilliers, chairman and manager of the NCMP, injects a drug to awaken a sedated cheetah after relocation.

Early in 2003, the WCMP was able to purchase a micro-light aircraft and radio collars. With these tools the researchers can track cheetahs and begin to understand their ranges and movements, particularly in the intensive game and stock ranching areas as well as across the South African borders with Zimbabwe and Botswana. Eventually the authorities will have to determine how to deal with illegal hunting and the continuous trading of illegally caught wild cheetahs. The information collected by the WCMP will provide valuable data in this process. Wildlife dealers who export cheetah skins to certain countries are a continuing part of the problem. Until government officials commit the necessary resources to combat these issues, cheetahs will continue to suffer.

Deon Cilliers uses the National Cheetah Management Program micro-light to scout for free-ranging cheetahs in the Limpopo Province.

Kelly Wilson meets farmers to gather accurate census information in the North West and Limpopo Provinces.

De Wildt has spearheaded the next phase of the program by organizing an extensive census of the wild cheetah population occurring on farmlands in South Africa. The census will cover an area of over eight million hectares (nineteen million, seven hundred thousand acres) and will likely take up to five years to complete. The census is extremely important because there is no existing data that can provide accurate information on the numbers of free-ranging cheetahs in the Limpopo, North West and Northern Cape Provinces in South Africa. Without accurate data, it is impossible to make informed decisions or develop long-term strategic goals. Compounding the need for a census is the fact that farmers seldom report when cheetahs are shot. For example, the official statistics for 2001-2002 in the Limpopo Province showed four official recordings of cheetahs being killed. Investigations have revealed that during that same time frame, at least thirty-three cheetahs were illegally shot in the Thabazimbi area alone, which is but a small fraction of the province.

Proposal for South African Cheetah Population Census in the Limpopo Province

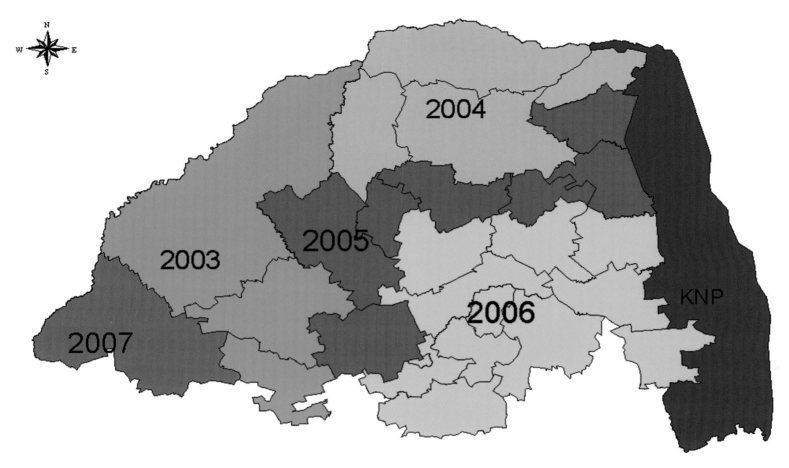

The Limpopo Province has been divided into sections for the collection of census data.

Community organization, compensation for farmers and ranchers, and the collection of data from the first cheetah census will help save wild cheetahs in South Africa. As the program gains momentum, it will provide important data for decision makers who will ultimately develop policies that will be needed to save South Africa's cheetahs.

The Wild Cheetah Management Program

The wild cheetah is fast becoming a rare species. Free-roaming cheetahs prey on farm and ranch animals, and in an effort to protect their livelihood, farmers have little alternative but to kill the cheetahs. The De Wildt Cheetah and Wildlife Trust is working to solve this problem by bringing together a group of farmers, conservationists, NGO's and academic institutions to develop a national cheetah management plan. The future of this species hangs in the balance. We need your help to tip the scales in favor of the cheetah.

To learn more about De Wildt and programs such as the Wild Cheetah Management Project in South Africa, the Reach for the Wild project, and the Cheetah Adoption Program contact:

De Wildt Cheetah and Wildlife Trust
P.O. Box 16 • De Wildt, Pretoria 0251
SOUTH AFRICA
Phone/Fax: 011.27.12.504.1921
Email: cheetah@dewildt.org.za
www.dewildt.org.za

In the United States, tax deductible
contributions can be sent to:
**The International Cheetah
Conservation Foundation**
P.O.Box 4508
Decatur, IL 62525

This information is provided through funding from the Howard G. Buffett Foundation.

These advertisements are part of the campaign 'Fading Spots: A Race Against Time', implemented by The De Wildt Cheetah and Wildlife Trust. The campaign is a call to action and has raised awareness and funding for the National Cheetah Management Program and the census program currently underway in South Africa.

Adopt-A-Cheetah

By adopting a cheetah at De Wildt Cheetah and Wildlife Trust, you will help support the daily operations that maintain De Wildt's cheetah population. This program allows individuals or families to contribute to the cost of a chosen animal's veterinary care, it's food, and the maintenance of it's environment. Recognition is given and a certificate of adoption is issued. Various levels of participation are available and each provides the same return; a huge reward and a better opportunity to save the world's cheetahs.

To learn more about De Wildt and programs such as the Cheetah Adoption Program, the Wild Cheetah Management Project in South Africa, and the Reach for the Wild project contact:

De Wildt Cheetah and Wildlife Trust
P.O. Box 16 • De Wildt, Pretoria 0251
SOUTH AFRICA
Phone/Fax: 011.27.12.504.1921
Email: cheetah@dewildt.org.za
www.dewildt.org.za

In the United States, tax deductible
contributions can be sent to:
**The International Cheetah
Conservation Foundation**
P.O.Box 4508
Decatur, IL 62525

This information is provided through funding from the Howard G. Buffett Foundation.

As the NCMP expands, the requirements for infrastructure also grow. De Wildt has partnered with the Nature Conservation Trust (NCT) of South Africa to provide additional resources. The NCT has established the Jubatus Cheetah Reserve, comprised of 5,000 hectares (12,000 acres) in the Limpopo Province. The primary objectives of the reserve are to support the NCMP by providing cheetah holding facilities, to extend De Wildt's research, and to enhance the possibilities of maintaining sustainable cheetah populations in South Africa.

The two unrelated male cheetahs released on the Jubatus Cheetah Reserve successfully bonded after about three months. They were originally kept separate in two adjoining pens. After they became more familiar with each other, they were allowed access to one another. The final step in bonding was to release them into a 1 hectare (2.5 acre) enclosure to determine if they would stay together or separate when put into a larger area. The bonding was accomplished prior to their release onto 1,100 hectares (2,718 acres).

Jubatus Cheetah Reserve currently has appropriate holding areas for twenty cheetahs. This provides the NCMP with facilities to hold rescued cheetahs in the heart of the problem area until they can be permanently relocated to a game reserve. The Jubatus Cheetah Reserve also provides overflow facilities for De Wildt and has plans to expand the amount of cheetah enclosures in the future to support the needs of the NCMP, WCMP and the De Wildt Captive Breeding Program. Other objectives of the reserve also include the provision of large open areas to expand De Wildt's research into the free-ranging cheetah's behavior.

Two temporary residents of Jubatus try their skills at wrestling.

A thorn is an inconvenience to this cheetah. He quickly forgets about it a few minutes later when a herd of impala approach.

The first requirement at Jubatus was to rehabilitate the land. Most of the land had previously been used for livestock feeding, leaving it overgrazed and in poor condition. With the support of environmental advisors and the Nature Conservation Department of the Limpopo Province, a set of environmental and developmental objectives was established for the reserve.

The original project on Jubatus was to establish the minimum land requirements for sustaining free-ranging cheetahs in the Limpopo Province. The results of this research will shape the policy of the Nature Conservation Department when issuing permits for smaller area game farms wanting to include cheetahs on their properties. Prior to the release of the first cheetahs, an assessment of the carrying capacity of the land was completed, and appropriate prey species were introduced, watering points were developed and the required fencing was constructed.

The first release of cheetahs on Jubatus combined two different challenges. A cheetah rescued from the wild when it was about four months old was bonded with a captive-born cheetah when they were both about fourteen months of age. It was unknown if the young cheetah from the wild would possess the necessary instincts to hunt and kill, and perhaps more importantly, whether or not the captive-born cheetah could learn to kill from such an inexperienced companion. The two cheetahs were released in August of 2002, and studies of their progress have provided answers regarding their ability to adapt to free-ranging conditions.

A number of challenging events faced the staff responsible for the cheetahs after their release. The wild born cheetah immediately made successful kills, however, they were sporadic at first. Therefore, human intervention was required for the first few months. Initially it appeared that the captive-born cheetah did not possess enough palate strength to rip open the carcass of the prey. He also did not immediately make the transition from being hand-fed to consuming freshly killed game. It was approximately three months after their release that the captive-born cheetah was first observed making a kill. Clearly the captive-born cheetah was slowly learning the necessary techniques to survive in the wild. Today, the two cheetahs have settled into a routine and have become more consistent with their hunting.

Rehabilitation of land is an important component of providing adequate space for free-ranging cheetahs. The first step at the reserve was to remove internal cattle fences and re-establish a healthy ecological system.

After a comfortable evening rest in the cool and soft sand of a dry river bed, this cheetah comes to life as the sun begins to rise.

This cat is on the prowl as a result of hunger, and stops for a quick drink.

					AMOUNT CONSUMED	TIME SPENT AT CARCASS
DATE	TIME	SPECIES	SEX	AGE		
13/08/2002	morning	impala	male	juvenile	back legs	1 day
14/08/2002	morning	blesbok	female	adult	back legs	1 day
18/08/2002	morning	impala	male	subadult	back legs	few hours
23/08/2002	afternoon	impala	male	adult	back legs	few hours
28/08/2002	morning	impala	male	juvenile	back legs, 1 shoulder, ate innards	1 day
31/08/2002	afternoon	impala	male	juvenile	back legs, shoulders	1 day
04/09/2002	morning	blesbok	female	adult	whole carcass	2 days
03/10/02002	afternoon	blesbok	female	adult	back legs, rib cage	2 days
15/10/2002	afternoon	blesbok	female	adult	whole carcass	2 days
21/10/2002	morning	blesbok	female	adult	back legs	few hours
30/10/2002	afternoon	blesbok	female	adult	back legs, 1 shoulder, rib cage	1 day
01/11/2002	morning	blesbok	female	adult	back legs, half of rib cage	1 day
03/11/2002	morning	blesbok	female	adult	back legs	1 day
11/11/2002	morning	blesbok	female	adult	3/4 of carcass	1 day
15/11/2002	morning	kudu	unknown	juvenile	whole carcass	few hours
25/11/2002	morning	blesbok	female	adult	3/4 of carcass	few hours
25/11/2002	morning	blesbok	unknown	lamb	whole carcass	few hours
29/11/2002	morning	blesbok	femal	adult	3/4 of carcass	1 day
08/12/2002	morning	kudu	unknown	calf	whole carcass	1 day
13/12/2002	afternoon	blesbok	female	adult	whole carcass	1 day
17/12/2002	morning	blesbok	female	adult	whole carcass	2 days
21/12/2002	no carcass found; did eat something					
25/12/2002	afternoon	blesbok	female	adult	whole carcass	2 days
31/12/2002	no carcass found; did eat something					
06/01/2003	afternoon	kudu	unknown	calf	whole carcass	1 day
10/01/2003	morning	blesbok	unknown	subadult	3/4 of carcass	1 day
17/01/2003	morning	blesbok	female	adult	3/4 of carcass	1 day
26/01/2003	morning	blesbok	unknown	lamb	3/4 of carcass	1 day

PREY TAKEN BY CHEETAHS ON JUBATUS FROM AUGUST 2002 TO JANUARY 2003

Above is a sample of the documentaion which is being recorded at the reserve. Combined with other data, it will provide information for wildlife authorities about releasing cheetahs on small game farms in the Limpopo Province.

The cheetahs are closely monitored on a daily basis to determine their habits, including prey selection and killing techniques. These observations, combined with others, will eventually reveal requirements for free-ranging cheetahs in the Limpopo Province. With these results, the Nature Conservation Department will be able to consider issuing permits for the release of cheetahs on game farms of varying sizes. It will also allow for the consideration of introducing additional captive-born cheetahs into wild conditions.

The future of the Jubatus Cheetah Reserve will depend heavily on the research priorities of De Wildt. Long-term goals include testing various approaches to breeding, analyzing variations in diets, observing king cheetahs in free-ranging conditions and studying technical data such as heart rate comparisons during resting, walking and immediately following a kill. Early results from current tests with captive cheetahs at the reserve appear to demonstrate that different feeding techniques, using freshly killed game rather than conventional rations, and timing the feedings to closely simulate wild conditions, may alleviate certain health concerns in captive cheetahs. Combining this type of research with both captive and free-ranging cheetahs may provide new solutions to old problems.

The collaboration between De Wildt and the Nature Conservation Trust will allow De Wildt to expand by using its premier reputation and success in captive breeding to help save free-roaming cheetahs in South Africa. The partnership between De Wildt and the NCT provides the opportunity to take De Wildt's mission a step further – to fulfill the highest goal in cheetah conservation: saving the wild cheetah from extinction. As conservation strategies continue to develop, De Wildt will be positioned to test and analyze the most effective ways to save cheetahs. Through successful breeding, participation in innovative initiatives, like the NCMP, and the opportunity to use the Jubatus Cheetah Reserve to learn and develop new ideas for sustaining cheetah populations, the future holds promise that this unique cat will survive.

It is not uncommon on the plains of Eastern Africa for cheetahs to climb onto vehicles. Here, one of the residents of Jubatus checks out a land rover.

Cheetahs get a large part of their required fluids through their kills. However, on a hot day they will take advantage of available water.

Farmers who are cheetah-friendly receive a sign, like the one above, to post on their property. The signs are distributed by the National Cheetah Management Program and are intended to help create awareness and support for the program.

When the day starts, the cheetahs are alert and the cubs stay close to their mother.

EPILOGUE

A DAY IN THE LIFE
OF A CHEETAH MOTHER

This story provides a brief glimpse of the vulnerability of cheetahs. Constantly fighting the battle to survive, the cheetah population faces the most difficult challenges of any African predator. Pushed to the edge of suitable habitat by stronger predators (lion, leopard, hyena and wild dog) cheetahs often find themselves in conflict with humans. A delicate balance exists for the long-term survival of the species.

A lion appears and briefly chases the cheetahs.

With the lion's arrival, the cheetah cubs are threatened. They quickly retreat as their mother briefly stands her ground.

The mother and cubs change directions to avoid another conflict with the male lion.

A DEADLY ENCOUNTER

June 10, 2001

A mother cheetah starts the day in search of food for her two cubs, one male and one female. Moving west, the cubs struggle to keep up the pace through the tall grass. Unknown to the mother cheetah, a group of young male lions is chasing one of the old resident male lions, pushing him in her direction. As the older male eludes the younger lions, he heads straight toward the cheetahs.

As the lion approaches the vicinity of the cheetahs, he is concealed by a small mound and the cheetahs are unaware of the lion's presence. When he spots the cheetahs, he breaks into a quick stride and the young cubs move fast, but the mother holds her ground momentarily to give a warning to the lion.

The odds are against the cheetahs. Under most circumstances the lion would pursue and kill at least one of the cheetahs, likely a cub. The mother would be helpless against a predator four times her size.

It seems that the reason the lion did not pursue the female or the cubs was that his own recent battle to survive left him tired and winded. Having skirted a close brush with death, and watching to assure the lion moves off, the mother heads in the opposite direction. A few hours later as the mother and cubs rest under a tree, a herd of impala begins to move straight towards the cheetahs. The mother crouches in a stalking position, and the cubs instinctively take cover while their mother initiates the hunt.

Keeping a sharp lookout, the mother spots a herd of impala.

The chase is on and the cheetah heads into her last turn at full speed.

The mother quickly assesses the impala herd and selects an individual. With a burst of speed, unmatched by any other animal, she bolts toward a male impala. Reversing the angle, the impala is now running for its life. As the pursuing cheetah rounds a corner at a speed of about eighty kilometers (fifty miles) per hour, the fleeing impala springs into the air.

Suddenly there is a huge thud and what we see next we are not prepared for, nor could we imagine. The mother, during the chase, clears a short log, and does not compensate for two broken branches. The rigid branches split the cheetah's sides as if a hunter has gutted her. She emerges with flesh and guts almost dragging on the ground.

The impala heads for the cover of bushes.

She stumbles forward, flops over, rolls, stands up momentarily and then with a heroic effort to stay up, falls to the ground. The look on her stunned face, like a soldier who just realizes he has been hit in combat, haunts me. Immediately I have two thoughts: can we put the mother out of her misery, and what to do about the cubs which are now destined to become orphans?

With the cheetah in close pursuit, the impala vanishes behind the bush which conceals the log.

We move the vehicle a short distance away from the mother, and the accompanying game ranger returns on foot to shoot the dying cheetah. I think of what the cubs might do at the sound of a gunshot. I make the decision to take the vehicle to where we had left the cubs. By the time the ranger returns to the mother she has taken her last few gasps of air. Even though there is no need to discharge the rifle, for some reason the cubs suddenly take off, as if they know something is wrong. Perhaps the amount of time that has elapsed without a call from their mother signals trouble.

The stumps of two broken branches bear fur from the cheetah, signs of a violent impact.

Now the cubs move rapidly in a southeast direction. I follow them, cautiously. The cubs proceed over the crest of the hill, and I lose sight of them. At the top of the hill I stop the vehicle and within a minute I hear them calling for their mother. I head in that direction and spot them. They are crossing the drainage line and hopefully they will not go far since I cannot follow across this terrain. They move up the hill opposite the ravine and stop. Now their constant calls for their mother might alert another predator, which would put them in imminent danger (only weeks before, lions killed two of three cubs from another female cheetah). The cubs look like they are going to stay in this area, not wanting to move too far from where they last saw their mother. I return and pick up the ranger, who doesn't need to explain what has happened: no gunshot means the mother died before he reached her.

The two cheetah cubs intermittently call for their mother, anxiously waiting to see if she will reappear.

Seconds after we hear the impact, the cheetah comes into view from behind the bush - she is disemboweled.

Within a few minutes the animal is lifeless.

The veterinary team prepares to tranquilize the cubs.

We radio for help. The immediate response comes from two other vehicles that help form a loose perimeter around the cubs. In about three hours the veterinary team arrives, ready to dart the cubs and move them to safety. They prepare the proper doses of Zolatol and load the rifle and aim for the female cub first. She doesn't move far and responds quickly to the drug. After about five minutes, the male is darted. He moves around in a large semicircle, not straying too far from his sister. He falls and gets back up at least half a dozen times, struggling and dragging his leg where the dart has hit. Finally, he goes down. The team starts to load the female, as the male is still too conscious to be moved. Placing the female in the Land Rover, one of the vets checks her pulse and breathing rate.

The cubs are moved to an area where they undergo tests for tuberculosis. Later they are relocated to The De Wildt Cheetah Wildlife Centre near Pretoria.

The sedated male cub is carefully carried to the vehicle.

The female cub is checked to ensure a satisfactory heartbeat.

Once darted, the female moves to her brother for reassurance.

The male cub puts up a fight against the drug, struggling for about five minutes before he succumbs.

A jackal surveys the cheetah carcass.

A few hours later, vultures devour the carcass in a matter of minutes.

Several weeks later, the cubs are safe at The De Wildt Cheetah and Wildlife Centre.

The loss of this female was difficult, but compounding the problem was that three weeks earlier a male cheetah in the same area broke its leg and had to be moved to a nearby breeding center. The loss of a female, a male and a total of four cubs from two litters within a month took a heavy toll on this cheetah population.

Cheetahs face increasing odds against survival. Built for speed, their bodies are vulnerable to injury. Low on the chain of predators, they lose kills to other animals that they cannot fend off. Cheetahs have little ability to defend themselves against leopards and lions, and as a result the mortality rate of cheetah cubs in the wild has been estimated as high as eighty percent. As cheetahs are pushed to the edge by predators and by man, we must recognize their vulnerability and act accordingly.

It is estimated that the cheetah species evolved five and a half million years ago. Left to its natural evolution, it is impossible to know how many more years this species would survive. It is clear, however, that man has interfered with this process. In a little more than a few decades we have eradicated the cheetah in a large part of its original territory, primarily through indiscriminate killing and habitat destruction.

Ancient Indian tribes had the foresight to view the impact of their judgements over a period of seven generations. They realized that their decisions would reach far into the future. That type of wisdom is rarely practiced today, resulting in policies, priorities and actions driven by short-term interests. The consequences of this current thinking have been devastating to nature worldwide.

Man's impact on the environment has begun to accelerate at a rate that the earth cannot sustain. Our destruction of species and habitat has created an imbalance in many natural systems. Through a network of intricate biodiverse ecosystems, nature has provided resources for almost every need. Frequently we destroy the very places, such as tropical rainforests, that hold natural solutions to future problems. This is a reckless and self-destructive pattern. As this generation becomes more aware of the impact of our behavior, it is incumbent upon us to re-evaluate the time frame in which we view the consequences of our actions.

The cheetah is but one species propelled toward this expedited demise. Consider five and a half million years of existence cut short by our lack of understanding and foresight. It is too late to assume that the cheetah will survive without our assistance. We must make a legitimate attempt to reverse the process we have initiated.

In a time when we possess the ability to technologically destroy all forms of life on our planet, surely we can find a way to preserve what the earth has provided. It is time to become accountable for what we have done. Accountability could begin by looking to the wisdom of the past and making decisions that will consider the results seven generations into the future. Maybe then species such as the cheetah will have a chance to survive.

Howard G. Buffett

Photographic Credits

HGB: Howard G. Buffett   **AVD**: Ann van Dyk

p.1:	**HGB**	pp.83-101:	**HGB**
p.3:	**HGB**	pp.102, 103:	**©Thomas D. Mangelsen**
p.4, 5:	**HGB**	pp.104-106:	**HGB**
p.7:	**HGB**	p.107:	**©Howard W. Buffett**
pp.9,10:	**HGB**	pp.108-123:	**HGB**
p.11:	**AVD**	p.124:	**HGB** (top left & bottom), **AVD** (top right)
pp.12-15:	**HGB**	p.125:	**AVD**
pp18-22:	**HGB**	p.126:	**AVD** (top), **HGB** (bottom)
p.23:	**AVD**	p.127:	**HGB** (top & bottom left), **AVD** (bottom right)
p.24:	**©John and Frank Craighead**	pp.128-133:	**HGB**
pp.25-30:	**HGB**	p.134:	**AVD**
p.31:	**AVD** (top), **HGB** (bottom)	p.135:	**©Dick Reucassel**
pp.32-37:	**HGB**	pp.136-140:	**AVD**
p.38:	**AVD**	p.141:	**HGB** (top), **AVD** (bottom)
pp.39-59:	**HGB**	pp.142, 143:	**AVD**
pp.60, 61:	**©Thomas D. Mangelsen**	pp.144-146:	**HGB**
pp.62-65:	**HGB**	p.147:	**AVD**
pp.66, 67:	**AVD**	p.148:	**HGB**
pp.68-72:	**HGB**	p.149:	**UNCREDITED**
p.73:	**AVD**	p.150	**AVD**
pp.74, 75:	**HGB**	pp.151-153:	**HGB**
pp.76, 77:	**AVD**	pp.156-161:	**HGB**
p.78:	**HGB** (top), **AVD** (bottom)	pp.163-183:	**HGB**
pp.79, 80:	**AVD**	p.185:	**AVD**
p.81:	**HGB**	pp.186, 187:	**HGB**
p.82:	**AVD**	Front Cover:	**HGB**
		Back Cover:	**HGB**

Text Credits

The primary text was compiled by Cynthia Kemp, in close collaboration with Ann van Dyk and Howard Buffett. Ann van Dyk contributed Chapter 8. Howard Buffett contributed Chapter 7, Chapter 9 and the Epilogue. Howard Buffett was the primary contributor for the captions. Editing was provided by Cynthia Kemp and Devon Buffett.

The De Wildt Cheetah and Wildlife Trust
P.O. Box 1756
Hartbeespoort, 0216
SOUTH AFRICA
Phone/Fax: 011.27.12.504.1921
E-mail: cheetah@dewildt.org.za

International Cheetah Conservation Foundation
P.O. Box 4508
Decatur, IL 62525
USA
Fax: 217.429.3988
E-mail: cheetahfoundation@yahoo.com

A slow walk to extinction, or a return to the wilderness?